To my wife

Vera

for her patience

and a special thanks to

The Canada Council

for its assistance

"PIONEER HOME" NANAIMO V.I   673 SELBY ST.
                                                    RANGER

First Printing: April, 1985
Second Printing: June, 1985
Third Printing: November, 1985

1

VANCOUVER ISLAND

Sketches and

Trip Notes

by Al Ranger

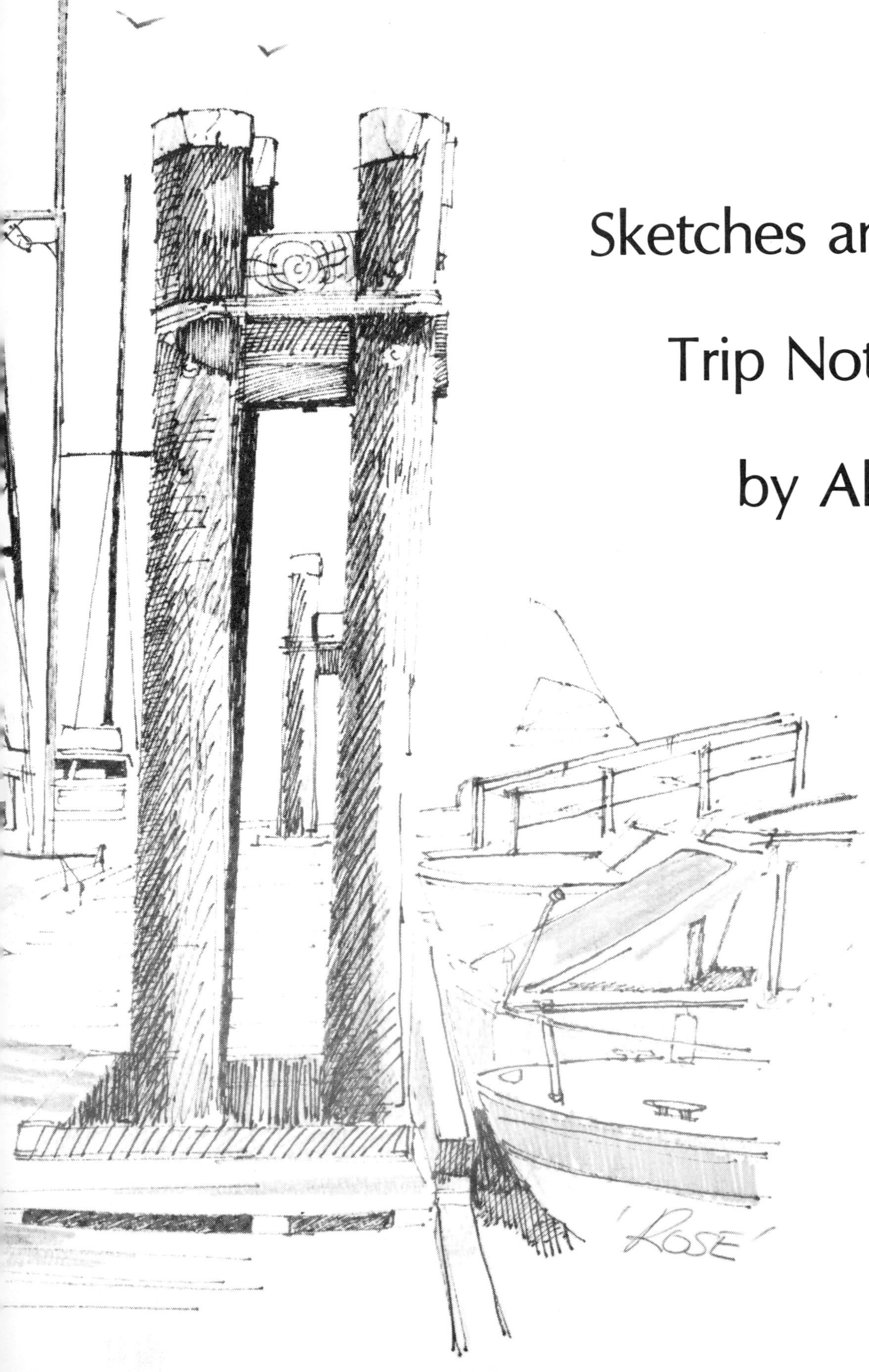

'Rose'

CAPE SCOTT PARK

PORT HARDY TO PRINCE RUPERT FERRY 491 KM

PORT HARDY

COAL HARBOUR

PORT McNEILL

ALERT BAY

TELEGRAPH COVE

KELSEY BAY. SAYWARD

PORT ALICE

ZEBALLOS

TAHSIS

GOLD RIVER

STRATHCONA PARK

FLORES ISLAND

KE
LA

TOFINO

LONG BEACH

UCLUELET

BROK
IS

VANCOUVER ISLAND MARMOT LIKE ITS ISLAND HOME, UNIQUE IN ALL THE WORLD.

VANCOUVER ISLAND

. . . Victoria to Cape Scott

Printed by Arrowmaker Graphics, Parksville, Vancouver Island.

ISBN 0-9692254-0-7 © COPYRIGHT 1985 - A.F. RANGER

Born in Nanaimo on Vancouver Island Al is a self-taught artist who began his full-time art career in 1979. His paintings are a part of many corporate and private collections in Canada and United States. He is represented in galleries in British Columbia and Alberta.

Running through Al's painting is an endless stream of sketching. It is his belief that the sketch is a statement complete unto itself. By assembling these sketches into a book form it is his hope that the total will hold an image . . . a glimpse of our Island.

THE PRODUCTION OF THIS BOOK HAS BEEN A LABOR
OF LOVE FOR TWO REASONS, ONE THERE IS NOTHING I
ENJOY MORE THAN SKETCHING AND SECONDLY THERE
IS NO PLACE I ENJOY MORE THAN THIS PACIFIC ISLAND
I MUST AT THE BEGINNING APOLOGIZE FOR ANY
WEAKNESSES IN THE PRINTED WORD. I AM ACCUSTOMED
TO CONVEYING MY THOUGHTS AND FEELINGS IN A GRAPHIC
MANNER AND SURROUNDING THESE GRAPHICS WITH
WORDS IS SOMETHING NEW TO ME. HOWEVER, IF THEY
TOGETHER EXPRESS "A LOVE OF PLACE" I HAVE BEEN
SUCCESSFUL

SINCE THIS BOOK WAS PULLED TOGETHER OVER A
PERIOD OF YEARS I FOUND THAT WHEN IT WAS READY
FOR THE PRINTING PRESS MANY OF THE SUBJECTS
WERE NO LONGER STANDING AND IT BECAME APPARENT
TO ME THAT OUR ISLAND WAS QUICKLY CHANGING,
CHANGE OF COURSE IS NECESSARY BUT IT DOES COME
WITH SOME LOSS. THE LOSS SO NOTICEABLE TO ME IS
THE LOSS OF HEIRLOOMS LEFT US BY THE FIRST SETTLERS
OF OUR ISLAND

MANY OF THE ROUTES SUGGESTED IN THIS BOOK ARE
OFF THE MAIN ROAD, MOST BACK-ROAD ADVENTURERS
DERIVE GREAT PLEASURE IN EXPLORING SUCH LITTLE-
KNOWN PLACES AND THEY DELIGHT EVEN IN OCCASS-
IONALLY GETTING LOST

I'M SURE I HAVE MISSED MANY INTERESTING OFF
THE BEATEN TRACK ROUTES BUT YOU WILL FIND
ISLANDERS MORE THAN WILLING TO ADD SUGGESTIONS
AND LOCAL COLOR.

HAPPY WANDERING!

Al Ranger

VICTORIA - THE CAPITAL CITY

FEW CITIES IN THE WORLD OFFER SO MUCH TO SEE IN SUCH A SMALL AREA AS OUR CAPITAL CITY VICTORIA AND THE BEAUTY OF IT IS, WITH ONE OF THE WORLDS MOST IDYLLIC CLIMATES YOU CAN ENJOY HER BEAUTY YEAR ROUND. NOWHERE ELSE ON THE WEST COAST OF NORTH AMERICA DO YOU FIND THE OLD WORLD CHARM AND ELEGANCE OF THIS CITY. BORN AS A HUDSONS BAY FORT, THEN BURSTING WITH GOLD SEEKERS OUTFITTING FOR THE CARIBOO AND FINALLY THE REFINEMENT OF A CAPITAL CITY DIRECTING THE AFFAIRS OF ONE OF CANADAS LARGEST AND RICHEST PROVINCES.

VICTORIA'S CASTLES

CRAIGDARROCH CASTLE

CRAIGDARROCH CASTLE IS A DREAM REALIZED.
IN 1851 ROBERT DUNSMUIR PROMISED HIS WIFE
IF SHE ACCOMPANIED HIM TO VANCOUVER ISLAND
HE WOULD MAKE A FORTUNE AND BUILD HER A
CASTLE. HE DID BOTH.
ROBERT WORKED FOR THE
HUDSONS BAY COMPANY
UNTIL HE DISCOVERED A
NEW SEAM OF COAL
AND BECAME AN OVER-
NIGHT MILLIONAIRE. HE
DIED BEFORE CRAIGDARROCH
WAS COMPLETED. HIS
WIFE JOAN LIVED IN THE
CASTLE UNTIL HER DEATH
THE CASTLE IS NOW
OPEN TO THE PUBLIC

ROYAL ROADS
ESQUIMALT

ROYAL ROADS
ESQUIMALT

A BIT OF OLD ENGLAND

THE ANTIQUE SHOPS OF FORT STREET ARE A TRIP INTO THE PAST AND LOOK LIKE SOMETHING STRAIGHT OUT OF DICKENS. DON'T BE TOO SURPRISED IF YOU SEE AN "EBENEZER" OR "OLD FEZZIWIG" POPPING IN OR OUT OF ONE OF THEM. FOR A BREAK YOU'RE SURE TO FIND A SHOP OFFERING AFTERNOON TEA.

ANTIQUE SHOPS
FORT STREET
VICTORIA

GOVERNMENT ST.

EVERYWHERE THERE IS THAT OLD WORLD CHARM, TUDOR STYLING AND QUALITY GOODS

VICTORIAN HOMES

TIRED OF TODAYS SQUARE BOX HOMES?
DOES YOUR FANCY RUN MORE TO BAY,
BOW, DORMER OR GABLE WINDOWS, COLUMNS,
CAPTAINS WALKS, VERANDAS AND GINGER-
BREADING THEN YOU WILL LOVE WANDERING
THE RESIDENTIAL
AREAS OF VICTORIA.

MANY OF VICTORIA'S
FINE OLD HOMES HAVE
BEEN RESTORED AND
ARE NOW SERVING AS
BUSINESS OFFICES
BOTH FOR THE GOVERN-
MENT AND THE PRIVATE
SECTOR.

THE EMPRESS

SO REGAL IS HER BEARING THAT YOU FEEL YOU SHOULD BOW OR CURTSY WHEN COMING BEFORE HER. "THE EMPRESS" IS ONE OF A SERIES OF C.P.R. HOTELS BUILT TO GRACE SOME OF CANADA'S MOST BEAUTIFUL SETTINGS. IT IS AS THOUGH VICTORIA'S INNER HARBOUR WERE POSITIONED TO ACCOMODATE "THE EMPRESS" RATHER THAN THE OTHER WAY AROUND. EVEN THE PARLIAMENT BUILDINGS TAKE SECOND PLACE IN POSITION. THE RICH AND THE FAMOUS CONTINUE TO SAIL IN AND PRESENT THEMSELVES TO HER

VICTORIA HAS A VERY LARGE CHINESE POPULATION AND THEIR ANCESTORS PLAYED A VERY SIGNIFICANT ROLE IN THE DEVELOPMENT OF THE ISLAND. IF YOU DINE HERE YOU ARE SURE TO BE PLEASED FOR VICTORIA'S CHINESE RESTAURANTS HAVE A REPUTATION FOR EXCELLENCE

CHINATOWN
VICTORIA.

IN 1977 THE PROVINCE OF BRITISH COLUMBIA PASSED LEGISLATION TO PROVIDE PROTECTION FOR THE HERITAGE RESOURCES OF THE PROVINCE. THE HERITAGE CONSERVATION ACT ESTABLISHES FOR THE FIRST TIME THE BRITISH COLUMBIA HERITAGE TRUST ITS ROLE UNDER THE ACT IS" TO SUPPORT, ENCOURAGE AND FACILITATE THE CONSERVATION, MAINTENANCE AND RESTORATION OF HERITAGE PROPERTY IN THE PROVINCE. THE RESTORATION OF MANY OF VICTORIA'S BEAUTIFUL OLD BUILDINGS IS EVIDENCE OF THE SUCCESS OF THIS ACT.

THE CLOCK TOWER
CITY HALL

I FOUND THIS SHOP ATTRACTIVE AND IT WAS INTERESTING TO SEE THE TERM "TOBACCONIST" USED IT SEEMED A WORD WHICH HAD LONG SINCE BEEN DROPPED FROM OUR VOCABULARY

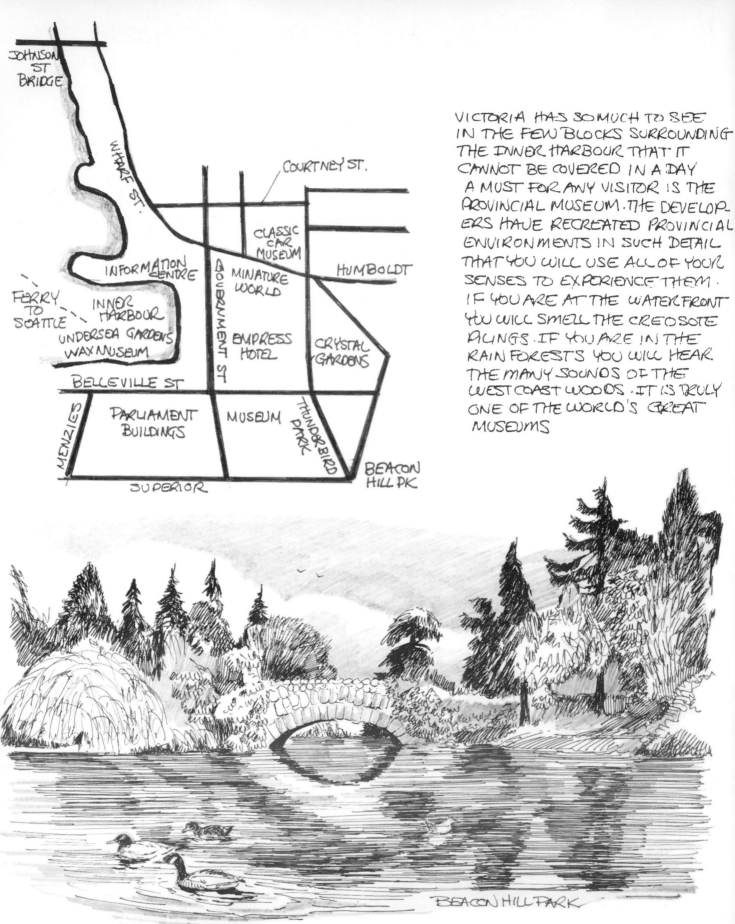

JOHNSON ST BRIDGE

WHARF ST.

COURTNEY ST.

CLASSIC CAR MUSEUM

INFORMATION CENTRE

HUMBOLDT

FERRY TO SEATTLE

INNER HARBOUR

MINATURE WORLD

GOVERNMENT ST.

UNDERSEA GARDENS
WAX MUSEUM

EMPRESS HOTEL

CRYSTAL GARDENS

BELLEVILLE ST

MENZIES

PARLIAMENT BUILDINGS

MUSEUM

THUNDERBIRD PARK

BEACON HILL PK

SUPERIOR

VICTORIA HAS SO MUCH TO SEE IN THE FEW BLOCKS SURROUNDING THE INNER HARBOUR THAT IT CANNOT BE COVERED IN A DAY. A MUST FOR ANY VISITOR IS THE PROVINCIAL MUSEUM. THE DEVELOPERS HAVE RECREATED PROVINCIAL ENVIRONMENTS IN SUCH DETAIL THAT YOU WILL USE ALL OF YOUR SENSES TO EXPERIENCE THEM. IF YOU ARE AT THE WATERFRONT YOU WILL SMELL THE CREOSOTE PILINGS. IF YOU ARE IN THE RAIN FORESTS YOU WILL HEAR THE MANY SOUNDS OF THE WEST COAST WOODS. IT IS TRULY ONE OF THE WORLD'S GREAT MUSEUMS

BEACON HILL PARK

JUST A SHORT DISTANCE FROM THE ACTIVITY OF THE INNER HARBOUR IS THE TRANQUILITY OF BEACON HILL PARK. THE PARK IS ALSO THE STARTING POINT FOR THE SCENIC MARINE DRIVE

18

THUNDERBIRD PARK.

THE POWERFUL NORTHWEST
COAST INDIAN ART WILL APPEAR
EVERYWHERE YOU TRAVEL ON
VANCOUVER ISLAND. IT IS
KNOWN AND RESPECTED BY
COLLECTORS AND ART HISTORIANS
AROUND THE WORLD. EVERY ARTIST
WHO IS EXPOSED TO IT IS AFFECTED
IN SOME WAY.
ONE OF THE WORLD'S LARGEST
COLLECTIONS IS HOUSED IN THE
PROVINCIAL MUSEUM AND IN
THUNDERBIRD PARK, ADJACENT
TO THE MUSEUM.

19

VICTORIA
YACHTING
FOUNDATION

THE CANADA 1, WHICH PLACED
FOURTH IN THE AMERICA CUP
SAILINGS MOST PRESTIGIOUS
RACE NOW CALLS VICTORIA
HOME

CANADA 1

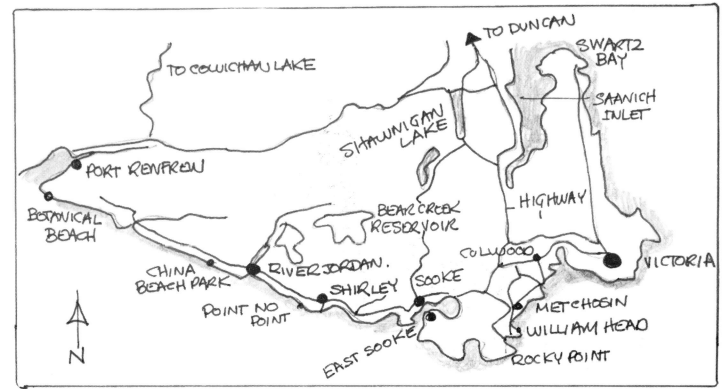

THE ROAD TO SOOKE WAS BUILT IN 1852 MAKING IT ONE OF THE OLDEST IN BRITISH COLUMBIA. IT WAS COMPLETED JUST NINE YEARS AFTER THE FOUNDING OF FORT VICTORIA. THE EXTENSION TO PORT RENFREW HOWEVER DIDN'T COME UNTIL 1957

TODAY IT PROVIDES AN INTERESTING EXCURSION FOR RESIDENTS OF VICTORIA AND A RELATIVELY QUICK ROUTE TO THE RUGGED WEST COAST OF THE ISLAND. ITS MOST WESTERLY POINT, BOTANICAL BEACH, RECEIVES THE FULL FORCE OF THE PACIFIC UNLIKE VICTORIA, WHICH IS SOMEWHAT SHELTERED BY WASHINGTON STATES, OLYMPIC PENINSULA. THE TRIP TO PORT RENFREW AND THE RETURN LOOP THROUGH THE FORESTS TO SHAWNIGAN LAKE IS A GOOD DAY'S EXCURSION FROM VICTORIA.

"FISGARD LIGHTHOUSE"
FORT RODD HILL
NATIONAL HISTORIC PARK

FISGARD LIGHTHOUSE IS LOCATED AT FORT RODD NATIONAL HISTORIC PARK NEAR COLWOOD. IT WAS BUILT IN 1860. THE FORT ITSELF WAS BUILT IN 1895 TO DEFEND THE BRITISH NAVY BASE IN ESQUIMALT HARBOUR

HER GUNS SILENT SHE NOW TREATS VISITORS TO 40 ACRES OF ROCKY PARKLAND. IN THE SPRING BLUE CAMAS, DOG TOOTH VIOLETS AND PINK SHOOTING STARS COVER THE WOODLAND FLOOR ARDENT BIRDWATCHERS MAY SIGHT THE BLACK OYSTERCATCHER

THE ATTRACTION TO ME HOWEVER, WAS THE LATE AFTERNOON SUN STRIKING THE STARK WHITE LIGHTHOUSE TOWER. A BACKGROUND OF FOG IN ESQUIMALT HARBOUR MADE IT AN EXCITING SKETCHING SUBJECT. VIEWED FROM THE TOP OF THE FORT OR AT THE ROCKY CAUSEWAY LEADING TO THE LIGHTHOUSE THIS IS A SKETCHING SUBJECT WHICH PROVIDES ENDLESS EXCELLENT COMPOSITIONS.

'ANNE HATHAWAY'S COTTAGE'
ESQUIMALT.

THIS FULL SIZE REPLICA OF ANNE HATHAWAYS
THATCHED COTTAGE IS LOCATED AT 429 LAMPSON
ST. OFF ESQUIMALT ROAD ON THE GROUNDS OF
THE OLDE ENGLAND INN. ANNE HATHAWAY
WAS THE WIFE OF WILLIAM SHAKESPEARE. A
GUIDED TOUR WILL ACQUAINT YOU WITH THE
LIFE STYLE OF THE SIXTEENTH CENTURY
IN THIS PERIOD PRIOR TO OUR PRESENT DAY DISHES
MEALS WERE SERVED ON BOARDS. WHICH WERE
SQUARE HENCE THE TERM "A SQUARE MEAL"
JUST ONE OF MANY INTERESTING BITS OF
TRIVIA RELATED BY THE GUIDE.

THIS OLD ANGLICAN CHURCH AT METCHOSIN IS
LOCATED JUST BEFORE THE GENERAL STORE
AT THE INTERSECTION OF HAPPY VALLEY ROAD
THE MOSSY, TWISTED GARRY OAKS SEEMED TO
FRAME HER SIMPLE CHARM.

ST. MARY THE VIRGIN.
ANGLICAN CHURCH.
METCHOSIN

RANGER '84

EAST SOOKE PARK.

WEST OF SOOKE

BOTANICAL BEACH

BOTANICAL BEACH.

ROFESSOR JOSEPHINE TILDEN FROM THE UNIVERSITY OF
NNESOTA WAS THE FIRST TO BRING THIS AREA TO
TE ATTENTION OF THOSE WISHING TO STUDY BOTANICAL
SPECIMENS OF THE PACIFIC
THE BEACH CONTAINS A GIANT SANDSTONE SHELF,
PERHAPS 500 FEET WIDE . WHEN THE TIDE GOES OUT
IT EXPOSES COUNTLESS POTHOLES SOME PEA SIZE
SOME AS BIG AS BATH TUBS BUT EACH CONTAINING
A CAPSULE OF ORGANIC LIFE

FISHERMANS
WHARF
SOOKE V.I.

POINT NO POINT

LOG SUSPENSION BRIDGE ON THE SAN
JUAN VALLEY ROAD TO SHAWNIGAN LAKE

JUST BEFORE PORT RENFREW THE ROAD BRANCHES
TO THE RIGHT TO THE LUMBER TOWNS AND ROADS
LEADING TO SHAWNIGAN AND COWICHAN LAKES

THE SAN JUAN RIVER ENTERS THE PACIFIC AT PORT
RENFREW. THE AREA WAS WELL KNOWN TO SPANISH
EXPLORERS. IN FACT PORT RENFREW WAS
ORIGINALLY CALLED PUERTO DE SAN JUAN. THE
AREA WAS THE SCENE OF MANY SMALL GOLD FINDS
BUT IT IS NOW THE COMPANY TOWN OF BRITISH
COLUMBIA FOREST PRODUCTS WHICH OWNS THE TIMBER
RIGHTS IN THE AREA.

THE SAANICH PENINSULA

MOST ISLAND RESIDENTS HAVE TRAVELED THE 20 MINUTE STRETCH OF HIGHWAY LINKING VICTORIA AND THE SWARTZ BAY FERRY TERMINAL BUT FEW HAVE TAKEN THE TIME TO WANDER THE GENTLE PASTORAL LANDSCAPE THAT LIES ON BOTH SIDES OF IT. PIONEERED FIRST BY THE ENGLISH SETTLERS WHO MOVED FARTHER OUT FROM FORT VICTORIA IT STILL HAS A DISTINCT ENGLISH AIR ABOUT IT.

THE ENGLISH SKYLARK, BROUGHT OVER BY HOME-SICK ENGLISH SETTLERS STILL SINGS OVER FIELDS OF WILD EASTER LILIES AND SHOOTING STARS COMPLETING THE PICTURE OF RURAL ENGLAND.

OUR LADY OF THE
ASSUMPTION
CATHOLIC CHURCH
WEST SAANICH RD.
RANGER 81

THIS BEAUTIFUL OLD CHURCH SAT CRISP AND WHITE IN THE LATE AFTERNOON SUNLIGHT. A WARM JULY BREEZE FROM THE SEA RUSTLED THE LONG DRIED GRASS AND DAISIES. THEY SEEMED MORE IN TUNE WITH HER THAN A MANICURED LAWN. THE WARM SUN AND SALT AIR MADE ME LINGER LONG AFTER COMPLETING THIS SKETCH.

RANGER

BEAVER LAKE STORE.
SAANICH.

REMEMBER THE DAYS WHEN CIGARETTE AND SODA POP COMPANIES TRIED TO OUT DO EACH OTHER WITH COLORFUL METAL SIGNS TO ADORN THE FACE AND SIDES OF CORNER GROCERY STORES. NOW MANY OF THOSE SIGNS ARE COLLECTORS ITEMS.

IF ON A HOT JULY DAY YOU FIND ONE OF THESE OASIS, PULL OVER, GO INSIDE AND GET YOURSELF AN ICE COLD SODA POP AND AFTER YOU HAVE EXCHANGED COMMENTS ON THE HEAT WAVE COME ON OUTSIDE, SET YOURSELF DOWN ON THE STEPS, IF THERE IS ROOM, AND REFLECT ON HOW NICE IT WAS WHEN ALL YOU HAD TO WORRY ABOUT WAS HOW YOU WERE GOING TO GET OUT TO THE LAKE FOR A SWIM.

PROSPECT LAKE MARKET
SAANICH

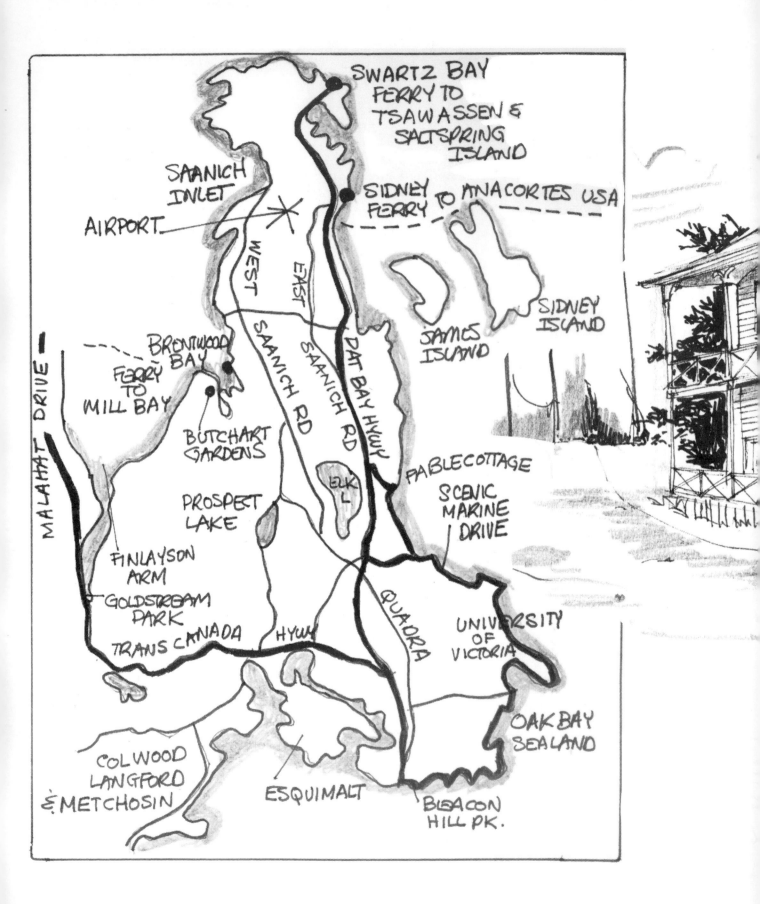

SWARTZ BAY
FERRY TO
TSAWASSEN &
SALTSPRING
ISLAND

SAANICH
INLET

AIRPORT

WEST

EAST

SIDNEY
FERRY TO ANACORTES USA

SIDNEY
ISLAND

JAMES
ISLAND

BRENTWOOD
BAY

FERRY
TO
MILL BAY

MALAHAT DRIVE

SAANICH RD

SAANICH RD

PAT BAY HWY

BUTCHART
GARDENS

PROSPECT
LAKE

ELK
L.

FABLE COTTAGE

SCENIC
MARINE
DRIVE

FINLAYSON
ARM

GOLDSTREAM
PARK

TRANS CANADA

HWY

QUADRA

UNIVERSITY
OF
VICTORIA

OAK BAY
SEALAND

COLWOOD
LANGFORD
& METCHOSIN

ESQUIMALT

BEACON
HILL PK.

RAIRIE INN.
SAANICHTON.
RANGER '81

I ATTENDED GRADE ONE IN A SCHOOL ABOUT A BLOCK FROM THIS GRACEFUL OLD INN. THE SCHOOL ROOM HELD GRADES ONE TO SIX, A ROW OF DESKS FOR EACH GRADE. IT WAS MY FIRST TIME BACK IN FORTY YEARS. YOU CAN IMAGINE MY SURPRISE AND DELIGHT AS I DROVE OVER THE RISE TO THE LEFT OF THE INN. SHE WAS STILL THERE!

OLD HOUSE
SAANICH
PENINSULA

A FELLOW TOLD ME THE STORY OF THE HUGE TREES OF ST. STEPHENS. SEEMS A FATHER OF THE BRIDE WHO WAS TO BE MARRIED AT ST STEPHENS HAD THOUGHT THE CHURCH EXTERIOR TOO STARK FOR THE WEDDING CEREMONY SO HE DUG UP A COUPLE OF EVERGREENS AND PLANTED THEM IN FRONT FOR THE DAY NO ONE REMOVED THEM AFTER THE CEREMONY.

ST. STEPHENS
ANGLICAN CHURCH
1862

RANGER.

OLDEST CHURCH IN BC. ON ITS ORIGINAL SITE AND HOLDING UNBROKEN SERVICES.
WEST SAANICH.

35

VICTORIA TO COWICHAN BAY VIA SHAWNIGAN LAKE

SOON AFTER LEAVING VICTORIA THE ISLAND HIGHWAY DROPS SLIGHTLY INTO GOLDSTREAM PARK. GOLDSTREAM IS KNOWN FOR ITS ANNUAL COHO AND CHUM SALMON SPAWNING. PICTURESQUE TRAILS LEAD THROUGH 600 YEAR OLD DOUGLAS FIR AND WESTERN RED CEDAR. FERN, WESTERN TRILLIUM AND CALYPSO CARPET THE FLOWERING DOGWOOD TREES. MANY VARIETIES OF MOSS COVER THE FOREST FLOOR, ROCKY HILLSIDES AND HANG FROM THE BRANCHES OF THE EVERGREENS AND MAPLES.

THE MALAHAT DRIVE BEGINS SHORTLY AFTER GOLDSTREAM PARK WITH SUPERB VIEWS OF THE SAANICH PENINSULA, THE GULF ISLANDS, FINLAYSON ARM AND MT. BAKER IN WASHINGTON STATE. THE DUTCH LATCH A RESTAURANT WITH A WINDMILL OUT FRONT OFFERS EXCELLENT MEALS AND CERTAINLY ONE OF THE GREATEST VIEWS ON VANCOUVER ISLAND. WATCH FOR THE HIGHWAY SIGNS "VIEWPOINT AHEAD" AND BE PREPARED WITH FILM.

THE MALAHAT DRIVE ENDS AS YOU DESCEND INTO MILL BAY. A FERRY LEAVES THE BAY REGULARLY TO TAKE CARS AND PASSENGERS TO THE SAANICH PENINSULA.

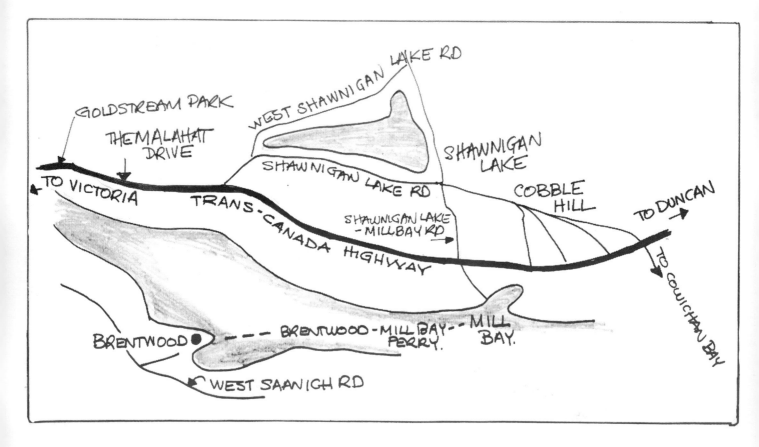

VIEW FROM THE MALAHAT.
FINLAYSON ARM.

TURN LEFT ONTO THE SHAWNIGAN LAKE - MILL BAY RD
SHAWNIGAN LAKE COULD BE STRAIGHT OUT OF THE MOVIE
"ON GOLDEN POND" QUIET, RESTFUL AND THE SORT OF SPOT
YOU'D DREAM OF SPENDING YOUR SUMMER VACATION OR
PERHAPS RETIRING TO WRITE THE GREAT CANADIAN
NOVEL.

SHAWNIGAN LAKE IS ALSO THE HOME OF THE SHAWNIGAN
LAKE BOYS SCHOOL, A VERY ENGLISH SCHOOL COMPLETE
WITH CRICKET, ROWING AND HIGH SCHOLASTIC
STANDINGS. THE HEART OF SHAWNIGAN LAKE VILLAGE
IS JERRY AND MARY ODEGAARDS GENERAL STORE
AND THE SHAWNIGAN GARAGE

SHAWNIGAN GARAGE
SHAWNIGAN LAKE

SHAWNIGAN LAKE
BOYS SCHOOL

AITKEN & FRASE
• GROCERIES
• MAGAZINE

AN ENGLISH BOYS PRIVATE SCHOOL TRANSPLANTED
IN ITS ENTIRETY IS EXACTLY WHAT THE SHAWNIGAN
LAKE BOY SCHOOL IS. I VISITED IT DURING CHRIST-
MAS BREAK. I WAS ALLOWED TO WANDER ITS
HALLS LINED WITH PICTURES OF THE ROWING TEAMS
OF THE 40'S, THE CRICKET TEAM, THE STERN FACED
HEADMASTER AND AN ARTICLE FROM AN OLD
COPY OF THE LONDON ILLUSTRATED NEWS PROMOTING
THE NEW SCHOOL IN THE COLONIES. WHEN I
LOOKED INTO ONE OF THE DORMS I WAS BROUGHT
BACK TO REALITY BY A BLACK LIGHT ROCK POSTER.

SHAWNIGAN LAKE
CORNER SHAWNIGAN LAKE RD
& SHAWNIGAN-MILL BAY RD.

COBBLE HILL

THE HEART OF THE LITTLE
COMMUNITY OF COBBLE HILL,
AT LEAST THE COMMERCIAL
HEART APPEARED TO BE THE
COBBLE HILL MARKET
TYPICAL OF MANY SMALL
ISLAND COMMUNITIES
THE MARKET SERVED
MANY MORE ROLES THAN
THE SIMPLE SALE OF
GOODS

COBBLE HILL
MARKET

COBBLE HILL HALL
COBBLE HILL

BINGO, DANCES, ELECTIONS, FALL FAIRS, COMMUNITY
MEETINGS. WEDDING RECEPTIONS ALL THESE AND
MORE ARE THE HERITAGE OF THE COBBLE HILL
HALL. LIKE SO MANY OF THE ISLANDS COMMUNITY
HALLS IT TOUCHED THE LIVES OF EACH AND EVERY
RESIDENT

THE BAKERY.
COBBLE HILL...

RANGER '81

AT A DISTANCE IT DIDN'T LOOK ANYTHING LIKE A BAKERY BUT IT WAS AND HAD BEEN FOR AGES. I FOUND IT BY STICKING MY NOSE INSIDE THE OPEN DOOR. THE SMELL OF WARM BREAD AND THE SACKS OF FLOUR INTRODUCED ME TO THE OLDEST BAKERY ON VANCOUVER ISLAND.

CONTINUE DOWN SHAWNIGAN LAKE ROAD TO THE ISLAND HIGHWAY (TRANS CANADA HYWY) AND CROSS AT THE LIGHT. THE ROAD NOW BECOMES THE COWICHAN BAY ROAD AND YOU ARE ON YOUR WAY TO THE SEA.

KINGSCOTE FARM.
COWICHAN BAY RD.

COWICHAN BAY

IF YOU HAVE COME TO VANCOUVER ISLAND TO
FISH COWICHAN BAY IS SURE TO BE A HIT. SPEND
SOME TIME AROUND THE PIER AND LEARN A BIT
ABOUT THE LOCAL CONDITIONS. THE OLDTIMERS,
THE ONES WITH THE COWICHAN INDIAN SWEATERS
OR TOQUES ON, WILL BE GLAD TO FILL YOU IN ON
HOW THE MOOCHING IS AT SANSUM NARROWS.
GETTING PROPERLY RIGGED FOR MOOCHING IS
THE FIRST LESSON TO LEARN. THERE'S ALWAYS
SOMEONE WHO WILL SHOW YOU.

IF YOU HAVE AN EYE FOR THE BEAUTY OF
NATIVE CARVING BE SURE TO LOOK INTO BETTY
WHITE'S SHOP. BETTY HAS SOME OF THE FINEST
MASKS, BOXES, RATTLES AND POLES CARVED BY
THE LOCAL SALISH INDIANS. BETTY'S SHOP IS SMALL
BUT FILLED WITH EXQUISITE GIFTS.

'THE MASTHEAD'
COWICHAN BAY.

DANGER '82

FISHING IN THE COWICHAN VALLEY

THE BEST SPOTS FOR SALMON ARE
COWICHAN BAY, SANSUM NARROWS
ACTIVE PASS - 20 MILES EAST
PORLIER PASS - 23 MILES NORTH
THE BEST TIMES TO CATCH SALMON
IN THESE AREAS ARE
SPRING SALMON - JUNE TO THE END
OF AUGUST
COHO - AUGUST TO OCTOBER
THE BEST SPOTS FOR TROUT FISHING
QUAMICHAN LAKE - CUTTHROAT 1-4 LBS
JAN — MARCH
SHAWNIGAN LAKE CUTTHROAT 8IN-15INS
SEPTEMBER — MARCH
SOMENOS LAKE - JANUARY TO MARCH
FISHING FOR CUTTHROAT AND RAINBOW
IN RIVERS FROM SEPTEMBER TO MAY
COWICHAN RIVER, KOKSILAH RIVER
& CHEMAINUS RIVER - NOVEMBER TO APRIL

43

ST. ANN'S CATHOLIC CHURCH IN COWICHAN
BAY WAS CONSECRATED IN 1870 BY BISHOP
DEMERS. THIS SOLID STONE STRUCTURE
BECAME KNOWN AS THE "BUTTER CHURCH"
BECAUSE FATHER RONDEAULT, ITS FIRST
PRIEST, ALSO AN ARDENT FARMER, PRODUCED
BUTTER, WHICH HE TRADED FOR LABOR ON THE
CHURCH. TEN YEARS AFTER ITS CONSTRUCTION
IT WAS ABANDONED IN FAVOR OF ANOTHER
ST. ANN'S, A FRAME STRUCTURE WHICH
STANDS CLOSE TO THE RESIDENTIAL SCHOOL,
TWO MILES AWAY.

RANGER '84

HUGE OLD MAPLE TREES SHADE A HERD OF
CATTLE IN THIS COWICHAN BAY PASTURE THIS
PICTURESQUE MAPLE GROVE IS A LANDMARK
AND PRESENTS A BLAZE OF COLOUR EACH OCTOBER

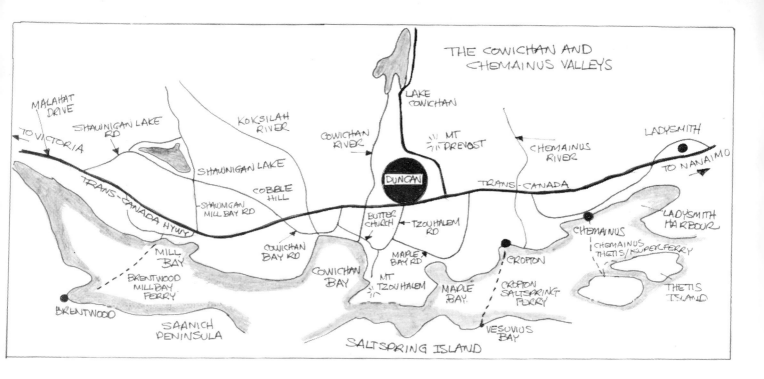

THE COWICHAN AND
CHEMAINUS VALLEYS

MALAHAT DRIVE
TO VICTORIA
SHAWNIGAN LAKE RD
KOKSILAH RIVER
LAKE COWICHAN
COWICHAN RIVER
MT PREVOST
LADYSMITH
TO NANAIMO
CHEMAINUS RIVER
TRANS-CANADA
SHAWNIGAN LAKE
COBBLE HILL
DUNCAN
TRANS-CANADA HWY
SHAWNIGAN MILL BAY RD
BUTTER CHURCH
TZOUHALEM RD
CHEMAINUS
LADYSMITH HARBOUR
MILL BAY
COWICHAN BAY RD
MAPLE BAY RD
CROFTON
CHEMAINUS THETIS/KUPER FERRY
BRENTWOOD MILLBAY FERRY
COWICHAN BAY
MT TZOUHALEM
MAPLE BAY
CROFTON SALTSPRING FERRY
THETIS ISLAND
BRENTWOOD
SAANICH PENINSULA
VESUVIUS BAY
SALTSPRING ISLAND

Ranger '84

Ranger '84

ST. ANN COWICHAN BAY. **45**

DUNCAN TO LADYSMITH

WIPPLETREE JUNCTION.
DUNCAN B.C.

ABOUT 8 MILES SOUTH OF DUNCAN YOU WILL
FIND AN INTERESTING ASSEMBLAGE OF TURN
OF THE CENTURY BUILDINGS HOUSING ANTIQUES,
LEATHER GOODS, SPINNING AND WEAVING CRAFTS, AN
EXOTIC ZOO A RESTAURANT AND MANY MORE
INTERESTING SHOPS MOST OF THE BUILDINGS
CAME FROM DUNCANS OLD CHINATOWN. THE
WOODEN SIDEWALKS AND COBBLESTONES HELP
CREATE A FEELING OF SHOPPING. IN AN ENVIRON-
MENT YOUR GRANDMOTHER MIGHT HAVE KNOWN.

WAGON WHEEL ANTIQUES
WHIPPLETREE JUNCTION

AS YOU APPROACH DUNCAN YOU ARE REMINDED
OF THE RICH HERITAGE OF THE SALISH INDIANS
ON THE RIGHT IS THE WORKSHOP OF MASTER
CARVER SIMON CHARLIE AN AREA WHERE HE
NOW INSTRUCTS YOUNG CARVERS, FARTHER ON
A LARGE BUILDING WITH TOTEM SUPPORTS IS
THE HOME OF HILLS INDIAN CRAFTS AND THE
LARGEST DISTRIBUTOR OF ORIGINAL WORLD
FAMOUS COWICHAN INDIAN SWEATERS. IN
THE PIONEER ERA SCOTTISH WOMEN INTRODUCED
INDIAN WOMEN TO THE DISTINCTIVE FAIR ISLES
METHOD OF KNITTING A STYLE ITSELF DATING
BACK CENTURIES IN SCOTLAND. ALREADY EXPERT

AT WORKING WITH MOUNTAIN GOAT WOOL THE
SALISH WOMEN TOOK TO KNITTING QUICKLY
INTRODUCING THEIR OWN NATIVE DESIGNS
MANY IMITATIONS ARE NOW ON THE MARKET
BE SURE TO CHECK AND SEE IF IT IS MADE
FROM HAND SPUN AND CARDED WOOL, FEEL
FOR LANOLYN CONTENT. IMITATIONS ARE
MADE IN PIECES, THE COWICHAN, KNITTED IN
THE ROUND FAIR ISLES STYLE IS A ONE
PIECE CONSTRUCTION. THEY ARE EXAMPLES
OF NATIVE CRAFTSMANSHIP EACH ONE
UNIQUE.

THE CITY OF DUNCAN HAS ITS SHARE
OF INTERESTING OLD HOMES. THIS
ONE ON THE CORNER OF TZOUHALEM
AND BRIAR ROADS CAUGHT MY EYE
THE OCTAGONAL TURRET ON THE SOUTH
SIDE WAS ESPECIALLY PLEASING

E & N RAILWAY
STATION
DUNCAN V.I.

RANGER '84

RANGER

CITY HALL DUNCAN . V.I

DUNCAN'S CITY HALL ON THE CORNER OF KENNETH AND
CRAIG STREETS IS ALMOST A DUPLICATE OF THE STONE
STRUCTURE WHICH SERVED AS NANAIMOS POST OFFICE
FOR YEARS.

DUNCAN. B.C.
RANGER

THE 100 ACRE B.C. FOREST MUSEUM LOCATED ON THE NORTHERN OUTSKIRTS OF DUNCAN IS A MUSEUM CHRONICLING THE HISTORY OF LOGGING ALONG THE BRITISH COLUMBIA COAST. THE STEAM LOCOMOTIVE IS THE MOST FAMOUS ATTRACTION WINDING THROUGH THE PARK, OUT OVER SOMENOS LAKE ON A 200 METER LONG TRESTLE AND PAUSING WHILE VISITORS TOUR THE MAIN LOG BUILDING. OTHER ATTRACTIONS INCLUDE A COMPLETE LOGGING CAMP, OLD TIME LOGGING TRUCKS, ORIGINAL STEAM DONKEYS AND "CRUMMIES" WHICH CARRIED THE LOGGERS FROM CAMP TO THE LOGGING SITE.

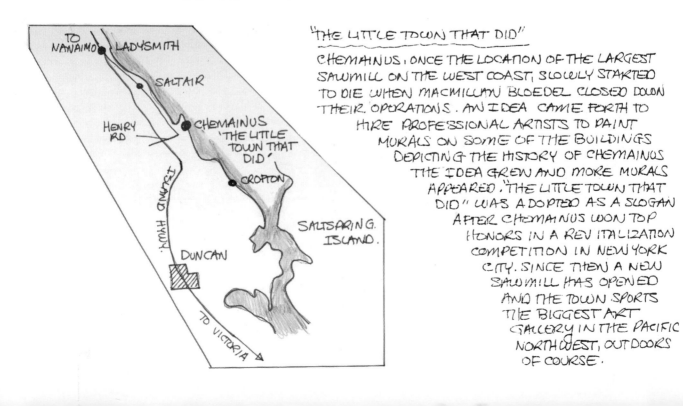

"THE LITTLE TOWN THAT DID"

CHEMAINUS, ONCE THE LOCATION OF THE LARGEST SAWMILL ON THE WEST COAST, SLOWLY STARTED TO DIE WHEN MACMILLAN BLOEDEL CLOSED DOWN THEIR OPERATIONS. AN IDEA CAME FORTH TO HIRE PROFESSIONAL ARTISTS TO PAINT MURALS ON SOME OF THE BUILDINGS DEPICTING THE HISTORY OF CHEMAINUS. THE IDEA GREW AND MORE MURALS APPEARED. "THE LITTLE TOWN THAT DID" WAS ADOPTED AS A SLOGAN AFTER CHEMAINUS WON TOP HONORS IN A REVITALIZATION COMPETITION IN NEW YORK CITY. SINCE THEN A NEW SAWMILL HAS OPENED AND THE TOWN SPORTS THE BIGGEST ART GALLERY IN THE PACIFIC NORTHWEST, OUTDOORS OF COURSE.

49

COWICHAN LAKE

THE RIVERSIDE INN
LAKE COWICHAN

RANGER

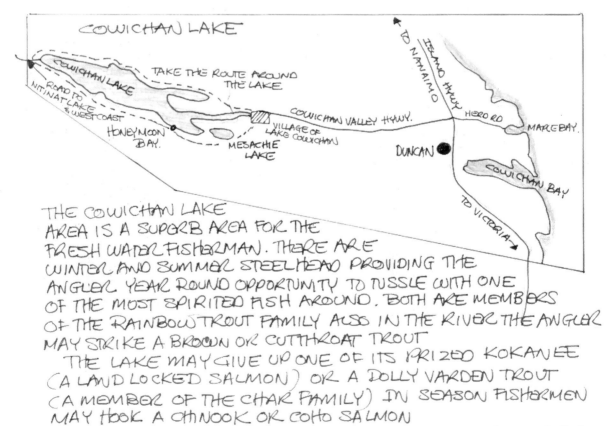

THE COWICHAN LAKE
AREA IS A SUPERB AREA FOR THE
FRESH WATER FISHERMAN. THERE ARE
WINTER AND SUMMER STEELHEAD PROVIDING THE
ANGLER YEAR ROUND OPPORTUNITY TO TUSSLE WITH ONE
OF THE MOST SPIRITED FISH AROUND. BOTH ARE MEMBERS
OF THE RAINBOW TROUT FAMILY ALSO IN THE RIVER THE ANGLER
MAY STRIKE A BROWN OR CUTTHROAT TROUT
   THE LAKE MAY GIVE UP ONE OF ITS PRIZED KOKANEE
(A LAND LOCKED SALMON) OR A DOLLY VARDEN TROUT
(A MEMBER OF THE CHAR FAMILY) IN SEASON FISHERMEN
MAY HOOK A CHINOOK OR COHO SALMON
   LOGGING IS THE LIFEBLOOD OF THE COWICHAN LAKE AREA
SO BE READY TO GIVE THE RIGHT OF WAY TO A HUGE
KENWORTH WITH A FULL LOAD.

SALTSPRING ISLAND

SALTSPRING ISLAND, THE LARGEST OF THE GULF ISLANDS CAN BE REACHED BY THREE FERRIES FROM CROFTON, JUST NORTH OF DUNCAN ON VANCOUVER ISLAND TO VESUVIUS ON THE WEST SIDE OF THE ISLAND. FROM SWARTZ BAY ON THE SAANICH PENINSULA TO FULFORD HARBOUR ON THE SOUTH END OF THE ISLAND AND FROM TSAWWASSEN ON THE MAINLAND TO LONG HARBOUR ON THE EAST COAST. THE ISLAND HAS A REPUTATION FOR ITS VERY RELAXED LIFESTYLE

RANGER/81

MOUATS MALL.
SALTSPRING. ISLAND

MOUAT'S MALL, SALTSPRING ISLANDS ANSWER TO THE
SHOPPING MALL CRAZE I MUST ADMIT IS THE ONLY
MALL I'VE EVER FELT COMFORTABLE AND RELAXED IN
NO PIPED IN MUSIC ONLY THE OCCASIONAL
CALL OF A GULL OR WAVES LAPPING AT
THE ROCKS BELOW. PLANK FLOORING
AND EVERYWHERE AN EXCEPTIONAL
VIEW OF GANGES HARBOUR.
INTERESTING ONE OF A KIND
SHOPS PERCHED ON PILINGS
AND ALL SEEMING TO BE
PART OF BOTH LAND AND
SEA.

MOUNT MAXWELL, SALTSPRING
ISLAND LAMB AND INTERESTING
DOWN-TO-EARTH FOLKS JUST
THREE OF THE INGREDIENTS THAT
MAKE THIS ISLAND UNIQUE

MT. MAXWELL
SALT SPRING. ISLAND.
RANGER/81

MOUAT, A NAME KNOWN THROUGHOUT THE ISLAND OF
SALT SPRING. JUST ONE OF THE FAMILIES THAT GUIDED
THE HISTORY OF THIS CHARMING ISLE.

VESUVIUS STORE
SALTSPRING ISLAND.

THIS INTERESTING MARKET SEEMS TO SPREAD
ITS WARES OUT TO MEET YOU AS YOU STEP FROM
THE FERRY AT VESUVIUS.

THE COMMUNITY HALL ON SALTSPRING ISLAND HAS
SERVED THE COMMUNITY FOR MORE YEARS THAN MOST
ISLANDERS CARE TO REMEMBER. WHILE ON THE ISLAND
I ATTENDED A SATURDAY NIGHT SPECIAL APPROPRIATELY
CALLED THE SMALL HALL BALL. A KITCHEN TABLE SERVED
AS THE BAR. THE FEATURED SINGER, A YOUNG GIRL
FORTUNATELY HAD A BOY FRIEND OR ADMIRER WITH A
LARGE FLASHLIGHT WHO SERVED AS LIGHTING DIRECTOR.
WITH A CEILING AS HIGH AS THE HALL WAS WIDE THE
SMALL HALL WAS JUST AS HIGH ON COMMUNITY SPIRIT.

ST. MARYS
FULFORD HARBOUR

RANGER '84

SALTSPRING ISLAND FARM

WILD BLACKBERRY
BUSHES SURROUND
THIS PICTURESQUE
LITTLE SHEEP RANCH
JUST OFF THE GANGES
FULFORD ROAD

ST. PAULS.
CATHOLIC.
CHURCH.
SALT SPRING ISLAND.

LADYSMITH TO NANAIMO

OLD POST OFFICE
LADYSMITH

LADYSMITH IS LIKE SAN FRANCISCO, ALL STREETS LEAD UP, STRAIGHT UP. JUST PUT YOUR CAR IN LOW GEAR AND CROSS YOUR FINGERS

AFTER LEAVING LADYSMITH YOU SOON COME TO IVY GREEN PROVINCIAL PARK, WHICH IS PART OF AN EXTENSIVE DELTA FRONTING ON A SILT-SAND BEACH AND TIDAL FLATS. A COUPLE OF MILES PAST THE PARK ENTRANCE A ROAD BRANCHES TO THE RIGHT. THIS LEADS TO THE CEDAR VALLEY AND YELLOW POINT AREAS, LAND WHICH IS BORDERED BY THE NANAIMO RIVER, A TERRIFIC STEELHEAD RIVER, AND THE POCKMARKED SANDSTONE SHORELINE OF THE COAST.

"OLD NO. 11"
COMOX LOGGING COMPANY.
LADYSMITH V.I

COOL, CLEAR
DRINKING WATER

ABOUT A HALF MILE NORTH OF IVY GREEN PARK ON THE LEFT SIDE OF THE HIGHWAY IS A FOUNTAIN WITH DELICIOUSLY COOL CLEAR DRINKING WATER.

THIS IMPRESSIVE OLD LOG LODGE SITS ON A BASE OF FLAT SANDSTONE HALF HIDDEN
BY GIANT GARRY OAKS AND DOUGLAS FIR. IT APPEARS TO HAVE ALWAYS BEEN A PART
OF THE YELLOW POINT LANDSCAPE. THE HUGE LIVING ROOM IS HEATED BY AN IMMENSE
STONE FIREPLACE. IF YOU CLIMB UP THE FACE OF THE FIREPLACE AND LOOK INTO A
HOLE BETWEEN THE GIANT RIVERROCKS YOU CAN SEE A HUMAN SKULL AT ITS
BASE. MR. HILL, THE OWNER WILL TELL YOU THE STORY OF HOW IT GOT THERE

WHEATSHEAF INN
CEDAR

HISTORICALLY, ONE OF THE OLDEST INNS IN BRITISH COLUMBIA THIS FORMER STAGE COACH
STOP WAS DESTROYED BY FIRE AND REBUILT IN 1926. LOCATED IN THE PICTURESQUE
CEDAR VALLEY ABOUT SEVEN MILES SOUTH OF NANAIMO IT IS A FAVORITE SPOT FOR
LOCALS. I VISITED IT ON A SUNDAY, THE INNS DAY OFF. THE OWNER NOTICED ME
SKETCHING AND INVITED ME IN FOR A TOUR, WITHOUT BEER OF COURSE.

ABOUT SEVEN MILES SOUTH OF NANAIMO THE MORDEN RD INTERSECTS THE TRANS-CANADA HIGHWAY. TURN RIGHT HERE AND THE MORDEN ROAD LEADS TO THE LAST STANDING RELIC OF THE ISLANDS COAL MINING ERA, "THE TIPPLE" OF THE OLD MORDEN MINE

"THE TIPPLE"
MORDEN MINE
SOUTH WELLINGTON

THE TINY ALMOST ISOLATED COMMUNITY OF EXTENSION WASN'T ALWAYS THIS WAY. IT ONCE SUPPORTED SEVEN DRINKING ESTABLISHMENTS, A MUST FOR THE THIRTY COALMINERS WHO LIVED THERE ONLY THE SLAG HILLS ARE LEFT AND A HANDFULL OF OLDTIMERS WHO WILL GLADLY TELL YOU TALES OF COAL, BOOZE, SOCCER, STRIKES, AND THE BIGGEST DARN STEELHEAD CAUGHT ON VANCOUVER ISLAND

59

NANAIMO - THE HUB CITY

NANAIMO BEGAN WHEN COAL TYEE, A LOCAL INDIAN
NOTICED WHITE MEN BURNING COAL IN FORT VICTORIA.
WHEN HE TIPPED THEM OFF TO BLACK ROCKS LIKE THAT
BACK HOME NANAIMO WAS BORN.

THE EARLIEST TRAILS FOLLOWED THE WATERFRONT
AND SINCE NO ONE SAW THE NEED TO STRAIGHTEN
THEM OUT AS TIME WENT ON, NANAIMO NOW HAS
THE MOST TWISTED MAIN STREET ON THE ISLAND OR
MAYBE THE PACIFIC COAST. HOWEVER IT IS ALSO LOADED
WITH CHARACTER.

HER BEAUTIFUL PROTECTED HARBOUR IS THE STARTING
POINT FOR THE NOW WORLD FAMOUS NANAIMO TO
VANCOUVER BATHTUB RACE. ONE OF THE THREE
PROTECTING ISLANDS IS NEWCASTLE A PROVINCIAL
PARK. THE OTHER TWO ARE PROTECTION ISLAND AND
GABRIOLA ISLAND.

HUDSON'S BAY CO
RANGE

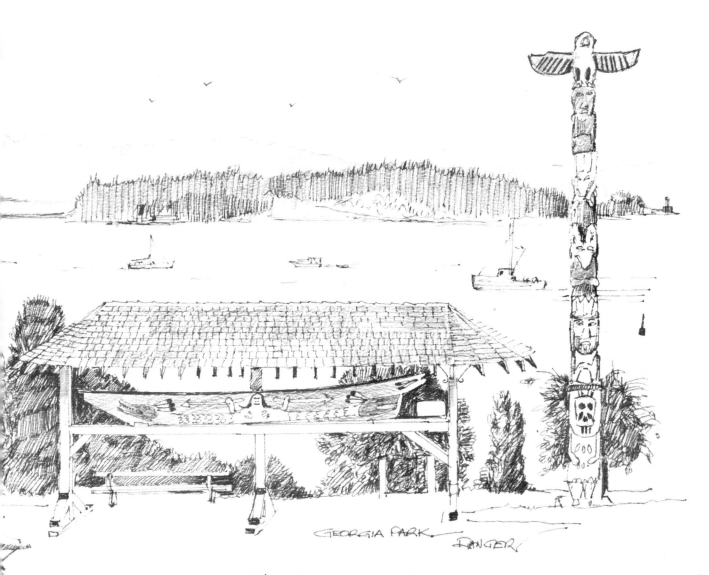

GEORGIA PARK. RANGER

THE BASTION, AN EARLY HUDSON BAY COMPANY
FORT STANDS GUARD OVER THE HARBOUR. BUILT
BY TWO FRENCH CANADIAN BUILDERS FOR THE
HUDSONS BAY COMPANY IT WAS NEVER USED FOR
ITS ORIGINAL PURPOSE, TO PROTECT THE EARLY
SETTLERS FROM HOSTILE INDIANS. IT NOW SERVES
AS A MUSEUM AND IS VISITED BY THOUSANDS.

GEORGIA PARK: THE STARTING POINT FOR THE ANNUAL
BATHTUB RACE
THIS PARK HAS A COMMANDING VIEW OF NANAIMOS
BEAUTIFUL HARBOUR. THE SCENE IS CONSTANTLY ALIVE
WITH FISHBOATS AND PLEASURE CRAFT TO THE LEFT
IS NEW CASTLE CHANNEL LEADING TO THE BRITISH
COLUMBIA FERRY TERMINAL. ON DISPLAY UNDER
THE SHELTER IS A FINE EXAMPLE OF AN EARLY
INDIAN CANOE.

102 FRY ST. NANAIMO

THIS OLD HOME IN NANAIMO'S SOUTH END NOW
LOOKS OUT TOWARD A SAWMILL, WHERE ONCE
STOOD ONE OF THE MOST PRODUCTIVE COAL
MINES ON THE COAST. A TUNNEL FROM THIS
MINE WENT UNDER NANAIMO HARBOUR COMING
UP AT PROTECTION ISLAND. IT IS SAID THAT
MINERS IN THE TUNNEL COULD HEAR SHIPS
OVERHEAD ENTERING OR LEAVING THE PORT.

NANAIMO BOAT BASIN IS ALWAYS FILLED
WITH SHIPS ; WHEN THE FISHING FLEET
LEAVES THE BASIN FILLS WITH VACATIONERS
IN YACHTS AND SAILBOATS FROM ALL OVER
THE WEST COAST.
THE STATELY OLD MALASPINA HOTEL ONCE
A LUXURIOUS CANADIAN PACIFIC RAILWAY
HOTEL HAS ONE OF THE BEST VIEWS OF
NANAIMO HARBOUR.

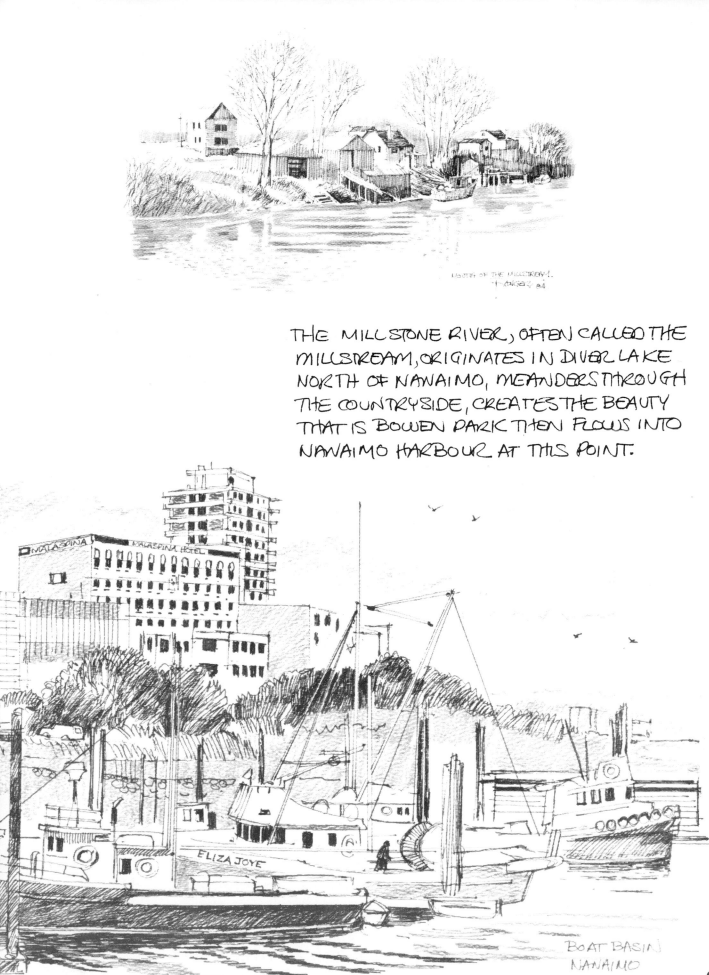

MOUTH OF THE MILLSTREAM.
T. HANGER 84

THE MILLSTONE RIVER, OFTEN CALLED THE
MILLSTREAM, ORIGINATES IN DIVER LAKE
NORTH OF NANAIMO, MEANDERS THROUGH
THE COUNTRYSIDE, CREATES THE BEAUTY
THAT IS BOWEN PARK THEN FLOWS INTO
NANAIMO HARBOUR AT THIS POINT.

ELIZA JOYE

BOAT BASIN
NANAIMO

AS THEY LEAVE DEPARTURE BAY
BOUND FOR HORSESHOE BAY THE
B.C. FERRIES TRAVEL THIS ROUTE
SAILING BETWEEN JESSE ISLAND
AND THE NORTHERN TIP OF
NEW CASTLE ISLAND.

BOWEN PARK

THIS HUGE FORESTED PARK IS LOCATED WITHIN THE
CITY, OFF BOWEN ROAD. IT CONTAINS, A DUCK POND,
PET FARM, SENIOR CITIZENS CENTRE, A CURLING
RINK, SWIMMING POOL AND A SOCCER FIELD BUT
WHAT IT IS MOST NOTED FOR IS THE BEAUTIFUL
MILL STREAM THAT MEANDERS THROUGH IT AND
THE FERN BANKED EARTHEN PATHS THAT LEAD
FROM QUIET POOL TO CASCADING WATERFALLS

SHACK ISLAND
PIPERS LAGOON.

PIPERS LAGOON, AN EXCITING SEA SIDE PARK, JUST
NORTH OF NANAIMO, OFF HAMMOND BAY ROAD OFFERS
BEAUTIFUL BEACHES, INTERESTING WALKS THROUGH
GNARLED OLD GARRY OAKS AND PICTURESQUE SMALL
ISLANDS WITH OLD SHACKS ONCE USED BY COMMERCIAL
FISHERMEN. THIS AREA IS A SKETCHERS OR PHOTOGRAPHERS
PARADISE.

"PREPARATION FOR THE SEASON"
BRECHIN POINT NANAIMO B.C.

THE PROPERTY FRONTING NEWCASTLE CHANNEL HAS ALL
THE CHARM OF SAN FRANCISCO'S WATERFRONT. HUGE
SEINERS UP ON WAYS BEING REFITTED FOR THE
FISHING SEASON, MARINE SUPPLY STORES, A FISH
CANNERY, THE LOCAL YACHT CLUB AND ONE OF A
KIND RESTAURANTS, ALL WITH THE BACKDROP OF
NEWCASTLE ISLAND PROVINCIAL PARK.

THE SOLID OLD NANAIMO COURT HOUSE
IS A BEAUTIFUL REMINDER OF THE CITY'S
HERITAGE. A QUARRY ON NEWCASTLE
ISLAND PROVIDED THE HUGE STONE
BLOCKS FOR ITS CONSTRUCTION. THE GREY
SHINGLE ROOF IS TOPPED WITH ORNATE
COPPER CAPS NOW EMERALD GREEN WITH
AGE. THE VERY PICTURE OF STEADFAST
JUSTICE, THE OLD BUILDING CONTINUES
TO SERVE THE COMMUNITY.

NANAIMO TO QUALICUM

LONG LAKE   RANGER

LANTZVILLE

LANTZVILLE HOTEL
RANGER

LANTZVILLE HOTEL··

BUILT BY ROSA CAILLET
THE DAUGHTER OF A
FRENCH HOTEL OWNER,
THE HOTEL WAS RUN BY
THE CAILLET FAMILY FOR
THREE GENERATIONS
THIS OLD LANDMARK,
WITH THE STALWART
GUIDANCE OF ARMAND
CAILLET RESISTED
CHANGE. IT REMAINS
ONE OF THE FEW ISLAND
HOTELS WITH THE ORIGINAL
ARCHITECTURAL DESIGN
OF ITS PERIOD.

I COULDN'T RESIST
SKETCHING THIS LITTLE
CHURCH TUCKED INTO
THE TREES. I ALSO
LIKE ITS UNIQUE SIGN
IT IS JUST BEYOND THE
LANTZVILLE HOTEL.

ST. PHILIPS
ANGLICAN CHURCH
LANTZVILLE V.I.

68

NANOOSE BAY.

I DID THIS SKETCH OF NANOOSE BAY FROM THE NANOOSE INDIAN RESERVE ON A GREY, CALM, FEBRUARY AFTERNOON ONLY THE DUCKS BROKE THE STILLNESS. ACROSS THE BAY LAY A CANADIAN NAVAL STATION. THE YELLOW CONNING TOWER OF A TRAINING SUBMARINE INTERJECTED COLOR INTO THE OTHERWISE BLACK AND WHITE SCENE.

Beachcomber MARINA

ONE OF THE FINE MARINAS WHICH CAN BE REACHED BY TURNING ONTO NORTHWEST BAY ROAD, JUST PAST THE ARLINGTON HOTEL. THE COUNTRYSIDE ALONG THIS ROAD MAKES IT AN INTERESTING SIDE TRIP. NORTHWEST BAY RD. REJOINS THE HIGHWAY BEFORE ENTERING PARKSVILLE

THE TWO OLD BARNS ILLUSTRATED HERE WERE LOCATED
ABOUT THREE MILES APART IN THE NANOOSE BAY AREA. THEY
ARE NO LONGER STANDING BUT I HAVE INCLUDED THEM TO
PRESERVE A RECORD OF THEIR BEAUTY. THEY WERE BOTH
CONSTRUCTED AROUND THE TURN OF THE CENTURY.

"IT IS POSSIBLE THAT MILLIONS NOW LIVING IN NORTH AMERICA
HAVE NEVER SEEN A BARN, LET ALONE BEEN IN ONE. IN THE
FORESEEABLE FUTURE THERE IS MORE THAN A POSSIBILITY
THAT FOR MANY, THE KIND OF BARN ILLUSTRATED ON THESE
PAGES WILL NOT BE THERE TO SEE. WHEN WE CONSIDER THE
EXPOSURE OF OUR OLD BARNS TO THE WINDS OF CHANGE, AS
WELL AS THOSE OTHER WINDS THAT HAVE BUFFETED THEM
FOR ALMOST A CENTURY   THE MARVEL IS THAT ANY ARE LEFT
FOR THOSE WHO WOULD TRY TO COMPREHEND THE SECRETS
THAT THEY HOLD"

CRAIG. BARN NANOOSE
1887-1984

DAWSON BARN.
DAWSON VALLEY
RANGER 82

71

Knox Heritage
Church
Parksville

RANGER

CRAIG HERITAGE PARK
LOCAL HISTORIANS HAVE ASSEMBLED MANY OF THE PIONEER BUILDINGS ON A SECTION OF WHAT WAS THE CRAIG FARM

THIS OLD "KNOX UNITED CHURCH" ONCE STOOD IN THE CORE AREA OF PARKSVILLE BUT WAS MOVED AND RESTORED IT NOW SERVES AS A MUSEUM.

RATHTREVOR PROVINCIAL PARK
RANGER

RATHTREVOR PROVINCIAL PARK IS THE BEGINNING OF "BEACH COUNTRY" FOLLOWED BY PARKSVILLE AND QUALICUM BEACH THE AREA IS THE MOST NOTED ON THE EAST COAST FOR SPLENDID WHITE SAND AND SAFE WADING BEACHES.

PARKSVILLE

PARKSVILLES BEAUTIFUL WIDE
SANDY BEACH IS IDEAL FOR THE
WHOLE FAMILY. THE DROP OFF IS
SO SLIGHT THAT YOUNGSTERS
ARE PERFECTLY SAFE TO WADE AND
BUILD SAND CASTLES. PARKSVILLE
BEACH IS BECOMING FAMOUS FOR
ITS ANNUAL JULY SAND CASTLE
CONTEST. THE CONTESTANTS BUILD
WORKS OF ART ' IN BETWEEN
TIDES. FOR A DAY OR AN HOUR
AT THE BEACH PARKSVILLE IS
PERFECT

"KWAKIUTL BEAR POLE"
CARVED BY JACK JAMES OF KWICKSUTAINEUK
BAND AT SIMOOM SOUND B.C.
PARKSVILLE B.C.

THE 'ROD AND GUN' ONE OF THE ISLANDS OLDEST HOTELS

E&N RAILWAY STATION
PARKSVILLE V.I
RANGER 81

THIS OLD ESQUIMALT AND NANAIMO
RAILWAY STATION HAS THE ONLY WATER
TOWER THAT I KNOW OF ON THE ISLAND,
A LEFT OVER FROM THE AGE OF STEAM.
THE STATION WAS USED IN THE MOVIE
"GREY FOX"

EAGLE CREST
RANGER

THE QUEEN OF ENGLAND HAS STAYED
IN THE OLD LODGE WHICH ONCE ADORNED
THIS PROPERTY. MANY OF THE OLD LOG
STRUCTURES NOW SURROUND AN

EXCELLENT NINE HOLE GOLF COURS
IT IS LOCATED ABOUT FIVE MILES NO
OF PARKSVILLE.

FISHBOATS AT FRENCH CREEK BOAT BASIN

FRENCH CREEK

WORK AND PLEASURE CRAFT SHARE THIS
PROTECTED GOVERNMENT BOAT BASIN.
AN EXCELLENT RESTAURANT WITH A SUPER
VIEW OF THE BOATS AND A CHEERFUL
NEIGHBOURHOOD PUB COMPLETE THIS
HARBOUR SCENE.

IN SEASON FRENCH CREEK
IS A SUPER SPOT TO BUY
LING COD, RED SNAPPER
PRAWNS AND SHRIMP.

FLOAT 6

CAROLYN

FEWER AND FEWER OLD
'DOUBLE ENDERS' LIKE
'THE CAROLYN' LEAVE
ISLAND WHARVES IN
PURSUIT OF SALMON
COD AND RED SNAPPER

"IRISH LASS"

QUALICUM BEACH

TAKE A BEAUTIFUL SWEEP OF BEACH,
A QUAINT VILLAGE CONVENIENTLY AWAY
FROM THE BEACH, A SUPERB GOLF
COURSE AND COVER IT WITH AN AIR
OF ENGLISH ARISTOCRACY AND YOU
HAVE QUALICUM.

QUALICUM IN INDIAN
MEANS "WHERE THE
DOG SALMON RUN"

SALISH BEAR POLE
CARVED BY SIMON CHARLIE

E&N RAILWAY STATION
QUALICUM BEACH
RANGER/ 81

QUALICUM BEACH

ESQUIMALT
AND
NANAIMO
RAILWAY

Qualicum College Inn
Qualicum Beach.

"THE QUALICUM COLLEGE INN"
ONCE A BOYS SCHOOL IN THE ENGLISH
TRADITION THIS BUILDING AND GROUNDS
NOW TREATS GUESTS TO CLOISTERED
PRIVACY AND EXCELLENT CUISINE STILL
IN THE ENGLISH TRADITION.

THIS CHARMING OLD LOG CHURCH IS ONE OF B.C'S MOST
PICTURESQUE. IT WAS BUILT IN 1894 BY 45 FARMERS
WHO USED OXEN TO HAUL THE LOGS. THE MARKERS IN
THE GRAVEYARD BEAR THE NAMES OF MANY OF THE
AREAS FIRST SETTLERS

ST. ANNES IS SITUATED
JUST WEST OF PARKSVILLES
ONLY COVERED SHOPPING MALL
IT IS SURROUNDED BY A HIGH
HEDGE MADE OF NATIVE
EVERGREENS.

WILLIAM H RATH

RATH

ST. ANNES ANGLICAN
CHURCH FRENCH CREEK.

RANGER '84

THE ROAD TO THE RIM

IF YOU LEAVE THE ISLAND HIGHWAY, HIGHWAY 19, JUST SOUTH OF PARKSVILLE YOU WILL HEAD WEST TOWARD THE PACIFIC. THIS ROUTE ENDING AT THE PACIFIC RIM NATIONAL PARK COVERS ABOUT 90 MILES AND TAKES YOU FROM THE SERENE EASTERN SHORES TO THE FIERCE, POWERFUL WEST COAST

5½ MILES AFTER LEAVING HIGHWAY 19 A SIGN WILL INDICATE THE ROAD TO ERRINGTON AND ENGLISHMAN RIVER FALLS PROVINCIAL PARK. IF IT HAPPENS TO BE A SUMMER SATURDAY MORNING YOU CAN TAKE IN THE ERRINGTON OUTDOOR MARKET OFFERING EVERYTHING FROM HOME MADE CRAFTS TO PERHAPS A FREE KITTEN AT THE GATE.

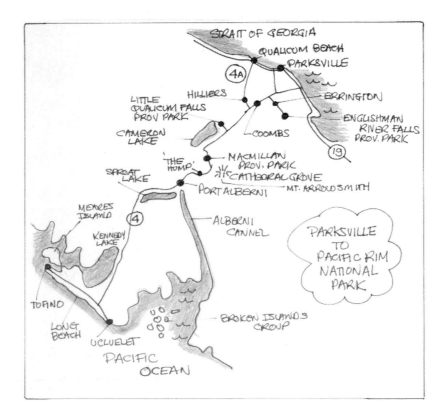

ERRINGTON AND ENGLISHMAN RIVER FALLS

ERRINGTON GENERAL STORE

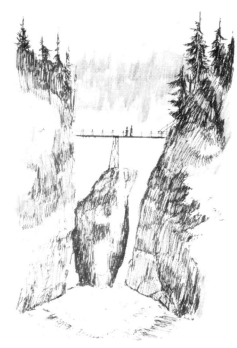

ENGLISHMAN RIVER
FALLS PROVINCIAL
PARK

EXCITING WATERFALLS
MASSIVE CEDAR FORESTS
LUSH FERN AND SALAL
UNDERGROWTH AND A
COOL RESTFUL PICNIC
AREA.

RANGER
'84

ST. MARY THE VIRGIN
ANGLICAN CHURCH
ERRINGTON V.I.

"GOATS ON THE ROOF"
COOMBS V.I.

BACK ON HIGHWAY 4, AND TWO MILES WEST IS THE LITTLE COMMUNITY OF COOMBS, HOME OF THE COOMBS COUNTRY OPERA AND ANNUAL BLUEGRASS FESTIVAL. A LARGE LOG BUILDING WITH GOATS FEEDING ON THE SOD-COVERED ROOF HOUSES A "SUPER" MARKET AND ONE OF THE BEST "BURGER AND FRIES" BARGAINS ON THE ISLAND. THE COUNTRY ATMOSPHERE OF ERRINGTON AND COOMBS IS SURE TO SLOW YOUR PACE.

WOODEN NICKEL
- HILLIERS. RANGER

3 OR 4 MILES
WEST ON YOUR
RIGHT A ROAD
LEADS TO LITTLE
QUALICUM FALLS
PROVINCIAL PARK
SIMILAR TO
ENGLISHMAN
RIVER FALLS IT
IS A TREMENDOUS
WATER SHOW

LITTLE QUALICUM FALLS
PROVINCIAL PARK

JUST A FEW MILES BEYOND LITTLE QUALICUM
FALLS PROVINCIAL PARK LIES CAMERON LAKE
ONE OF THE ISLAND'S MOST BEAUTIFUL LAKES
THE EARLY MORNING STILLNESS CREATES
AN ALMOST PERFECT MIRROR EFFECT REFLECTING
ICY BLUES AND VIBRANT GREENS ALMOST CERTAIN
TO MAKE YOU PULL OVER AND REACH FOR YOUR
CAMERA

AFTER CAMERON LAKE HIGHWAY 4 HEADS STRAIGHT INTO THE ISLAND'S ANSWER TO THE CALIFORNIA REDWOODS, MACMILLAN PROVINCIAL PARK, A 136 HECTARE PARCEL OF GIANT VIRGIN TIMBER SET ASIDE FOR YOUR ENJOYMENT. IT IS CLAIMED THAT ONE OF THESE GIANTS WOULD SUPPLY ENOUGH LUMBER TO BUILD SIX AVERAGE HOMES. BE SURE TO STOP AND WALK THE PATHS OF CATHEDRAL GROVE. IF YOU TAKE PICTURES BE SURE TO HAVE SOMEONE POSE IN FRONT OF THESE MONSTERS, OTHERWISE NO ONE BACK HOME WILL BELIEVE HOW BIG THEY REALLY ARE

PORT ALBERNI

AS YOU LEAVE CATHEDRAL GROVE HIGHWAY 4 STARTS THE
ASCENT TO THE TOP OF "THE HUMP" THEN DESCENDS INTO THE
ALBERNI VALLEY. AN EXCELLENT VIEW OF MT ARROWSMITH
CAN BE SEEN FROM THE TOP OF "THE HUMP"

"LADY ROSE"

IF IT FITS YOUR SCHEDULE YOU
MIGHT CONSIDER A CRUISE ON
THE "LADY ROSE" ONE OF THE
PACIFIC NORTHWESTS MOST
UNUSUAL AND PICTURESQUE SALT
WATER CRUISES, 90 MILES OF
WILDERNESS INCLUDING VIRGIN RAIN
FORESTS, ISLAND INLETS, WEST COAST
SETTLEMENTS AND POSSIBLY GREY OR
KILLER WHALES. THE LADY ROSE WAS
BUILT IN SCOTLAND AND SAILED OUT
TO BRITISH COLUMBIA UNDER HER OWN
POWER. SHE IS LICENSED FOR 100
PASSENGERS AND HAS A COMFORTABLE
LOUNGE AND COFFEE SHOP

T. ARROWSMITH
FROM "THE HUMP"
RANGER '84

TOWARD THE
MACKENZIE RANGE ON THE ROAD
TO THE WEST COAST

"THE KENNEDY
RIVER"
ON THE WAY TO
PACIFIC RIM NATIONAL PARK

AFTER LEAVING PORT ALBERNI YOU SOON ENCOUNTER SPROAT LAKE, A FAVORITE CAMPING AND FISHING SPOT, THE LAKE IS ALSO PART OF THE PROVINCIAL PARK NETWORK. THE HIGHWAY FOLLOWS THE LAKE ON ITS NORTHERN SHORE, THEN CROSSES THE TAYLOR RIVER AND HEADS IN MORE OF A SOUTHWEST DIRECTION. SOON YOU PICK UP THE KENNEDY RIVER WHICH DRAINS INTO KENNEDY LAKE. AFTER KENNEDY LAKE YOU WILL NOTICE A CHANGE IN THE FOREST GROWTH. THE LARGE FORKED YELLOW CEDARS APPEAR AND ALSO THE DWARF PINE, WHICH LOOKS LIKE SOMETHING OUT OF A JAPANESE BONSAI ARRANGEMENT SOON YOU REACH AN INTERSECTION TO THE RIGHT LIES THE PACIFIC RIM NATIONAL PARK AND TOFINO; TO THE LEFT THE VILLAGE OF UCLUELET.

LONG. BEACH

EVEN ON CALM DAYS THE
PERMANENTLY ARCHED
EVERGREENS TELL OF
PACIFIC STORMS AND
REMIND US THAT WE ARE
ON THE RIM OF A CONTINENT.

CHARACTERISTIC OF THE PACIFIC
RIM NATIONAL PARK ARE THE
GIANT YELLOW CEDAR, THEIR
FORKLIKE SILHOUETTES PIERCING
THE MOISTURE LADEN ATMOSPHERE

UCLUELET TO THE SOUTH IS A PICTURESQUE FISHING
VILLAGE. TOUR BOATS CAN BE HIRED TO TAKE YOU
OUT INTO THE PACIFIC WHERE YOU MAY VIEW GREY
OR KILLER WHALES. ANNUAL MIGRATION BRINGS
THOUSANDS SLOWLY BY IN MARCH AND APRIL
EN ROUTE FROM BREEDING AND CALFING GROUNDS
IN BAJA CALIFORNIA. OTHER SEA LIFE INCLUDES
STELLARS SEA LIONS, HARBOUR SEALS, RIVER OTTER
DOLPHINS AND PORPOISES.

UCLUELET

LONG BEACH

TWELVE MILES OF HARD PACKED SAND IS
THE MAJOR ATTRACTION. BUT APART FROM
THIS SPACIOUS BEACH WITH ROARING
SURF THERE IS A SPECIAL FEELING
SOMEHOW YOU KNOW YOU ARE STANDING
ON THE RIM OF A CONTINENT – NOTHING
SOLID OUT THERE UNTIL JAPAN. THE
WEATHER AFTER THOUSANDS OF MILES
OF OCEAN SEEMS TO SAVE ITS STRENGTH
FOR LONG BEACH. FISHING BOATS STAY WELL
OUT FROM THE COASTLINE. TREMENDOUS
BREAKERS THROW ALL MANNER OF THINGS
ONTO THIS BEACH: GLASS JAPANESE
FISHING FLOATS, A LIFE PRESERVER WITH
THE SHIPS NAME BARELY READABLE OR A
BOTTLE FROM A RUSSIAN SHIP. YOU'LL ENJOY
SEARCHING AMONG THE DRIFTWOOD FOR
YOUR FIND.

"A FORMER HYDROGRAPHIC SURVEY SHIP,
"THE CANADIAN PRINCESS" NOW OPERATES
AS A FLOATING HOTEL-CUM-CHARTER
FISHING AND NATURE CRUISE HEADQUARTERS
SHE IS DOCKED IN THE HEART OF UCLUELET

QUALICUM TO COMOX
INCLUDING LIGHTHOUSE COUNTRY

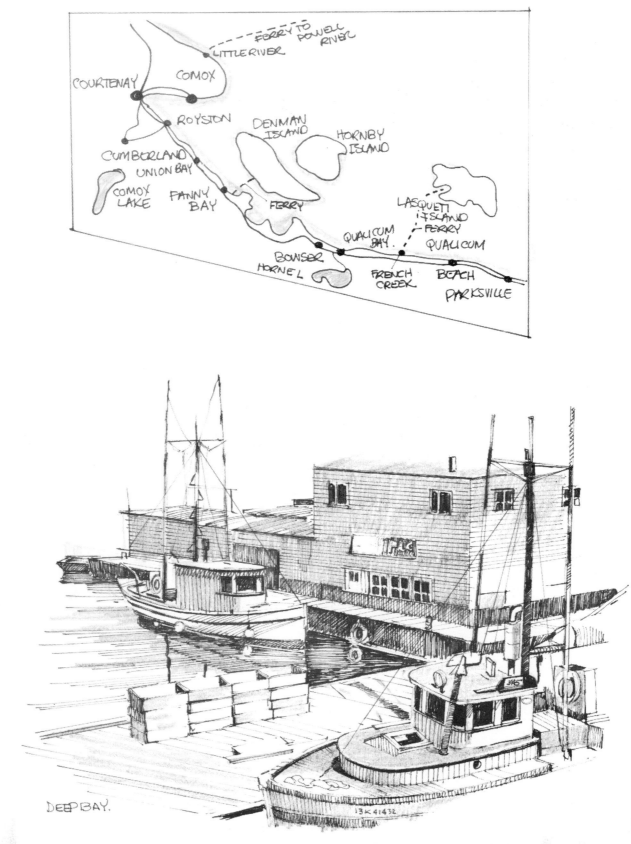

FERRY TO POWELL RIVER

LITTLE RIVER

COURTENAY

COMOX

ROYSTON

DENMAN ISLAND

HORNBY ISLAND

CUMBERLAND

UNION BAY

COMOX LAKE

FANNY BAY

FERRY

LASQUETI ISLAND FERRY

QUALICUM BAY

QUALICUM

BOWSER

HORNE L

FRENCH CREEK

BEACH

PARKSVILLE

PAC

DEEP BAY.

13 K 41432

BUILT IN SEATTLE IN 1908 THIS SHIP WAS ORIGINALLY DESIGNED TO BE A STEAM TRAWLER. IN 1930 SHE WAS RECHRISTENED `BRICO" AND BEGAN HER CAREER AS THE LAST OF THE CABLE-LAYING SHIPS PLYING B.C. WATERS. AS A CABLE SHIP SHE WAS NEVER OPERATED UNDER HER OWN POWER BUT WAS TOWED BY A PAIR OF TUGS NOW SHE SERVES AS A SEA-FOOD RESTAURANT AT FANNY BAY. AFTER SKETCHING HER I WENT ABOARD FOR A "WIMPEY BURGER"

MAC'S OYSTERS
FANNY BAY.   RANGER '81

BRICO

CUSTOMER
PARKING
ONLY

THE EAST COAST
BETWEEN QUALICUM
BAY AND UNION BAY
HAS LONG BEEN THE
OYSTER CAPITAL OF
VANCOUVER ISLAND
OYSTER LEASE SIGNS
CAN BE SEEN ALL
ALONG THIS AREA
ANYONE TRAVELING
THIS AREA SHOULD
BUY A SHUCKING
KNIFE AND TRY HIS
HAND AT SHUCKING
AND COOKING
OYSTERS OR FOR
THE PURIST
EATING THEM
RAW FROM THE
SHELL.

THE WATERFRONT THROUGH FANNY BAY AND OYSTER BAY SPARKLES WITH THE CRISP WHITE SHELLS OF OYSTERS. THIS OLD BUILDING WAS ONE OF THE CENTRES FOR OYSTER FARMING ALTHOUGH IT APPEARED ABANDONED THE SMELL OF THE SHELLS STILL REMAINED.

THE POST OFFICE
UNION BAY

UNION BAY WAS ONCE A COAL SHIPPING TERMINAL FOR THE RICH CUMBERLAND MINES. THE OLD COAL WHARF IS GONE. A FEW PIECES OF ARCHITECTURE PAY TRIBUTE TO ITS HISTORICAL IMPORTANCE A SMALL OLD JAIL HOUSE NOW SERVES AS A GIFT SHOP FEATURING LOCAL ARTS THIS STATELY OLD BRICK POST OFFICE CONTINUES ITS ROLE IN THE SMALL COMMUNITY

CUMBERLAND... A TRIP BACK IN TIME.

RANGER/81   CUMBERLAND. V.I.
ROWS OF OLD MINERS HOMES LOOK ACROSS
DUNSMUIR AVENUE IN THE OLD TOWN

CUMBERLAND HAS ALWAY BEEN ASSOCIATED WITH COAL MINING. COAL WAS DISCOVERED IN THE AREA IN 1864. IN THE 1880's THE COAL BARON ROBERT DUNSMUIR BOUGHT ALL COAL INTEREST IN THE AREA CHINESE, JAPANESE AND BLACKS WERE BROUGHT IN TO WORK THE MINES. ONE OF THE LARGEST CHINATOWNS IN NORTH AMERICA WAS LOCATED IN CUMBERLAND. AS YOU DRIVE INTO TOWN YOU ARE SURE TO HAVE THE FEELING OF GOING BACK IN TIME CUMBERLAND HAS SOME HOW RESISTED CHANGE..

THIS INLET REACHES RIGHT UP INTO THE CITY OF COURTENAY GIVING IT A SPECIAL APPEAL AND PROVIDING VERY SAFE MOORAGE FOR THE FISHING AND PLEASURE CRAFT.

COURTENAY ...

BASE CAMP FOR TWO OF BRITISH COLUMBIA'S FINEST
SKI AREAS MOUNT WASHINGTON AND FORBIDDEN
PLATEAU. FLOWER LINED BOULEVARDS LEAD INTO THIS
CHARMING ISLAND CITY ..

THE OLD HOUSE
RESTAURANT
COURTENAY

THE COURTENAY HOTEL.

HOTEL COURTENAY HOTEL

BOAT TRAILERS FOR RENT ft DOUBLE SLE 4 SALE

DATSUN

RANGER '84

WELCOME TO THE OLD HOUSE

I STOPPED TO SKETCH THIS ATTRACTIVE
VINE COVERED RESTAURANT. IT SEEMED
SO SKETCHABLE. I LATER FOUND OUT
THEIR FOOD WAS ALSO GREAT.

ST. ANDREWS ANGLICAN 1873
CHURCH
COURTENAY. B.C.

RANGER

PIONEER HOME
COMOX. V.I
RANGER '84

PIONEER HOME AT
COMOX

IN 1873 REVEREND
XAVIER WILLEMAR
OPENED THIS BEAUTIFUL
CHURCH TO HIS FLOCK
IN THE COMOX VALLEY
A SCHOOL-CHAPEL AND
BURIAL GROUND WERE
OPENED AT THE SAME
TIME. THIS IS THE
SECOND CHURCH, THE
ORIGINAL WAS LOG.
THE BELL WAS SALVAGED
FROM THE AUSTRALIAN
SHIP "LADY BLACKWOOD"
WHICH WENT AGROUND
NEAR PORT ALBERNI

MEMORIAL POLE TO DAVE MARTIN
COMOX V.I

THIS INDIAN COMMUNITY HOUSE CAN BE SEEN FROM THE
HIGHWAY BETWEEN COURTENAY AND COMOX. THE
COMMUNITY CENTRE IS THE FOCAL POINT FOR THE
POTLATCH. MADE COMPLETELY OF CEDAR IT HAS A LARGE
HOLE IN THE ROOF TO LET OUT SMOKE. THE POLE
IN FRONT WAS CARVED BY CHIEF MUNGO MARTIN OF
THE PORT HARDY AREA.

COMOX

THE FILBERG LODGE, ORIGINALLY THE HOME OF R.J. FILBERG, AND HIS WIFE FLORENCE IS NOW OPEN TO THE PUBLIC. MR. FILBERG, OF COMOX LOGGING COMPANY, EMPLOYED LOCAL CRAFTS-MAN WILLIAM HAGARTY AND HIS SON JOE TO FASHION A UNIQUE HOME USING NATIVE WOODS THE HAND HEWN POSTS AND BEAMS, WEATHER-ED SHAKE ROOF, WITH ITS CURVED GABLE AND THE GRACEFUL STONE CHIMNEY BLEND BEAUTIFULLY WITH THE ARTISTICALLY LAND-SCAPED GROUNDS.

RANGER '82

RANGER '84

FILBERG LODGE
COMOX V.I.

THE LORNE HOTEL:
THE OLDEST HOTEL IN
BRITISH COLUMBIA.
ITS WIDE VERANDA ADDS
A REFLECTIVE NOTE TO
THE DEVELOPING DOWN-
TOWN CORE OF COMOX
AFTER COMPLETING THE
SKETCH I FOUND
INTERIOR AND THE BEER
REFRESHING . . .

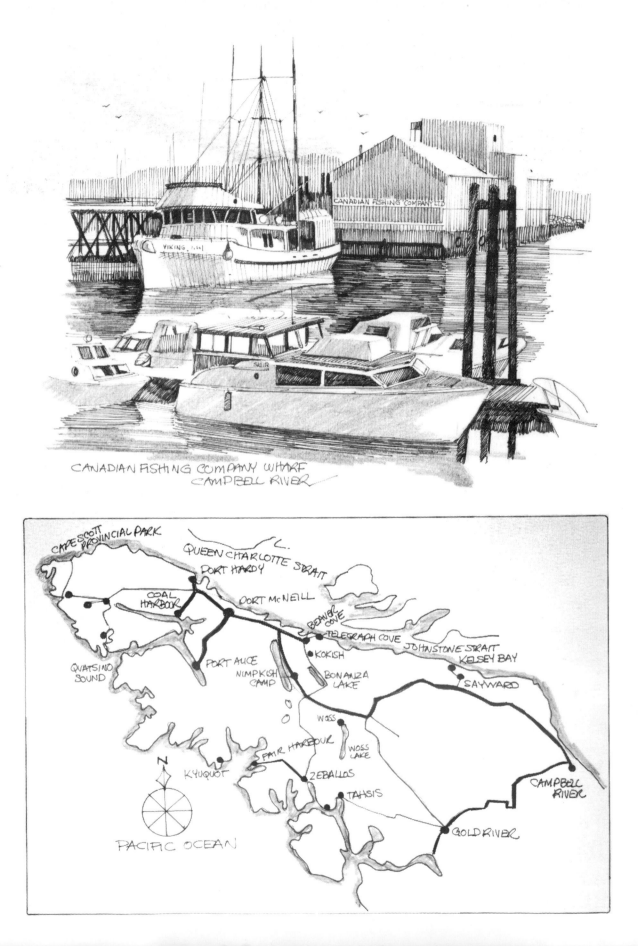

CANADIAN FISHING COMPANY WHARF
CAMPBELL RIVER

THE CAPE MUDGE LIGHTHOUSE ON QUADRA ISLAND LOOKS ACROSS THE ACTIVITY OF DISCOVERY PASSAGE TO THE CITY OF CAMPBELL RIVER A KWAKIUTL NATIVE MUSEUM DISPLAYS AN ARRAY OF POTLATCH ARTIFACTS FROM THE PAST ON THE CAPE MUDGE INDIAN RESERVE

CAPE MUDGE LIGHTHOUSE QUADRA ISLAND

THE KWAKIUTL NATIVE MUSEUM ON THE CAPE MUDGE RESERVE DISPLAYS AN EXCELLENT ARRAY OF POTLATCH ARTIFACTS.

CAPE MUDGE INDIAN RESERVE QUADRA ISLAND

RANGER '84

REBECCA SPIT
QUADRA ISLAND.

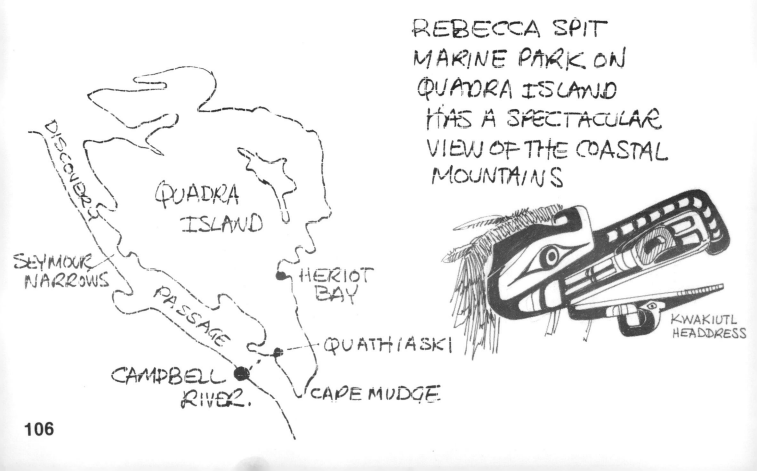

REBECCA SPIT
MARINE PARK ON
QUADRA ISLAND
HAS A SPECTACULAR
VIEW OF THE COASTAL
MOUNTAINS

DISCOVERY

QUADRA
ISLAND

SEYMOUR
NARROWS

PASSAGE

HERIOT
BAY

QUATHIASKI

CAMPBELL
RIVER.

CAPE MUDGE

KWAKIUTL
HEADDRESS

LOGGERS BOOT NOW SERVES AS A PLANTER

THE CABLE COOK HOUSE AT SAYWARD HAS A TERRIFIC COLLECTION OF PIONEER LOGGING HARDWARE ALSO LOCATED ON THE SAME PROPERTY IS A PIONEER AND LOGGING MUSEUM DEPICTING THE PROGRESSION OF THE AREA FROM FARMING TO EARLY LOGGING TO PRESENT DAY LOGGING OPERATIONS. THE COOKHOUSE WALLS ARE COVERED WITH USED LOGGING CABLE FRANCES AND GLEN DUNCAN HAVE BROUGHT THIS INTERESTING COLLECTION TOGETHER

KELSEY BAY.

172 KM / PORT HARDY.

1 KM

Ø KM

CABLE COOKHOUSE

NEW SALMON RIVER BRIDGE

CAMPBELL RIVER

MT. KUSAM PROVIDES A DRAMATIC BACKGROUND FOR AN OLD WHARF WHICH ONCE SERVED A FERRY TO PRINCE RUPERT. A SMALL GROUP OF PLEASURE AND FISHBOATS IS PROOF THAT KELSEY BAY DID NOT DIE WHEN THE FERRIES STOPPED.

THE ELDERLEY MRS KOSIE, OWNER OF THE KELSEY BAY
STORE NOTICED ME SKETCHING HER STORE AND
INVITED ME IN AFTER I HAD COMPLETED THE SKETCH
I LEARNED THAT SHE HAD BOUGHT THE BUSINESS IN
1958. A FERRY HAD RUN FROM THE WHARF NEAR HER
STORE TO PORT HARDY AND ALERT BAY BUT IT HAD
BEEN DISCONTINUED. I WONDERED HOW HER SMALL
STORE COULD NOW SURVIVE.

THIS HUGE "A" FRAME STRUCTURE, NOW UNUSED
STANDS NEXT TO AN EVEN LARGER NEW METAL
MACHINE SHOP IN THE CANADIAN FOREST PRODUCTS
NIMPKISH LOGGING CAMP. HUGE TIMBERS FORM
THE FRAMEWORK AND ALTHOUGH SOME OF THE
PLANKING IS MISSING IT APPEARS AS STURDY
AS THE DAY IT WAS ERECTED

SS CAMP
NADIAN FOREST PRODUCTS
GLEWOOD DIVISION.

RANGER 81.

"STEAM LOCOMOTIVE USED FOR LOG HAULING
WOSS CAMP.

I WAS ADVISED BY AN OLD LOGGER TO
VISIT WOSS CAMP, A DIVISION OF
CANADIAN FOREST PRODUCTS. HE
SAID IT WOULD SOON BE CLOSED. I
SKETCHED BUNKHOUSES BUILT ON
SKIDS FOR EASY MOVEMENT AND
AN OLD STEAM LOCOMOTIVE,
ONE COULD STILL GET THE FEELING
OF HOW IT MUST HAVE BEEN. A
CAMP BUSTLING WITH THE SOUND
OF CALK BOOTS ON PLANK FLOORS
AND THE PIERCING SOUND OF THE
OLD STEAM "LOCY" STILL SEEMED
TO ECHO OFF THE SCARRED
MOUNTAINSIDES

TELEGRAPH COVE

LIKE A HOLLYWOOD MOVIE SET THE TINY COMMUNITY
OF TELEGRAPH COVE IS SET APART FROM THE PROGRESS
OF THE REST OF THE NORTH ISLAND. ITS OLD HOMES
LINKED TO A COMMON BOARDWALK SEEM TO SYMBOLIZE
THE BOND THAT LINKS THE MILLWORKERS THAT INHABIT
THIS COVE

THE OWNER OF THE GENERAL STORE FILLED ME IN ON
ITS HISTORY. AS THE NAME IMPLIES THE COVE STARTED OUT
AS A TELEGRAPH STATION. SALTED SALMON EXPORT
TO JAPAN REQUIRED WOODEN BOX CONTAINERS
SO A SMALL SAWMILL WAS STARTED HERE TO
MANUFACTURE THESE BOXES. DURING THE SECOND
WORLD WAR THE COVE WAS TAKEN OVER BY THE
AIR FORCE. AFTER THE WAR THE SAWMILL CONTINUED.
TODAY IT IS SURROUNDED BY THE GIANTS OF THE B.C.
LUMBER INDUSTRY BUT IT CONTINUES TO OPERATE
INDEPENDENTLY. THERE IS TALK OF A TRAILER CAMP-
SITE TO BE LOCATED NEXT TO THE COVE OR PERHAPS
IT IS A REALITY. I HOPE THAT TELEGRAPH COVE CAN
WITH STAND THE TIGHTENING BOUNDARIES OF PROGRESS

TELEGRAPH COVE

RANGER 81

SAWMILL AT
TELEGRAPH COVE.

COVE SAWMILL
TELEGRAPH COVE

AS I SKETCHED THIS OLD SAWMILL
THE SHRIEK OF THE NOON HOUR
WHISTLE FILLED THE TINY COVE.
IMMEDIATELY ALL THE
MACHINERY WAS SHUT
DOWN AND A HUSH FELL
OVER THE LITTLE
COMMUNITY

↑ VILLAGE-
ON-STILTS

AN OLD
FASHIONED
BOARD WALK
RUNS THE
LENGTH OF THE
WATERFRONT
THE UNDERSEA WORLD
IS A SCUBA DIVERS
DREAM.

111

OLD HOME
TELEGRAPH
COVE.

POTTED PLANTS ARTISTICALLY
ARRANGED AGAINST AN OLD
TWELVE PANE WINDOW, FIRE
WOOD STACKED NEATLY AGAINST
A WEATHERED, SHINGLED SHED
WORK CLOTHES DRYING ON A
LINE STRETCHED FROM A BACK
PORCH TO THE SHED
VIGNETTES OF TELEGRAPH COVE

BEAVER COVE V.1
RANGER/81

BEAVER COVE

OLD HOMES DOT THE HIGH TIDE
LINE OF THIS SISTER COVE TO
TELEGRAPH COVE

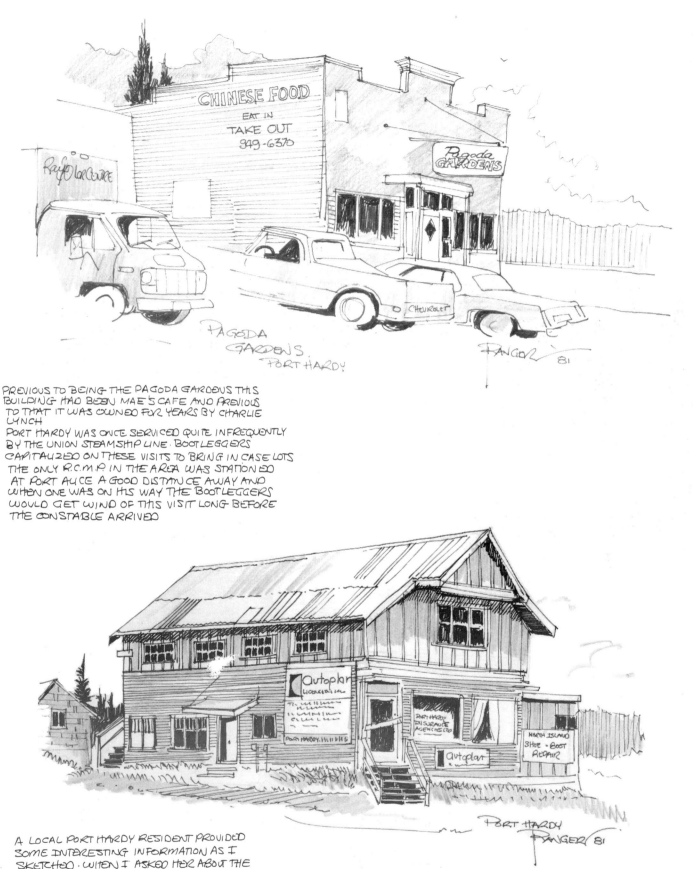

PREVIOUS TO BEING THE PAGODA GARDENS THIS
BUILDING HAD BEEN MAE'S CAFE AND PREVIOUS
TO THAT IT WAS OWNED FOR YEARS BY CHARLIE
LYNCH
PORT HARDY WAS ONCE SERVICED QUITE INFREQUENTLY
BY THE UNION STEAMSHIP LINE. BOOTLEGGERS
CAPITALIZED ON THESE VISITS TO BRING IN CASE LOTS
THE ONLY R.C.M.P. IN THE AREA WAS STATIONED
AT PORT ALICE A GOOD DISTANCE AWAY AND
WHEN ONE WAS ON HIS WAY THE BOOTLEGGERS
WOULD GET WIND OF THIS VISIT LONG BEFORE
THE CONSTABLE ARRIVED

A LOCAL PORT HARDY RESIDENT PROVIDED
SOME INTERESTING INFORMATION AS I
SKETCHED. WHEN I ASKED HER ABOUT THE
BUILDING I WAS SKETCHING SHE TOLD
ME IT HAD ORIGINALLY BEEN OWNED BY
A MINING COMPANY AND LATER AS A SCHOOL
AND NOW AS AN OFFICE BUILDING
SHE SLIPPED IN A TOUCH OF HUMOR WHEN
SHE TOLD OF HOW THE FOUNDING FATHER
OF PORT HARDY HAD RENTED THE BUILDING
OUT FOR 15 YEARS BEFORE IT WAS DISCOVERED
THAT HE WAS NOT EVEN THE OWNER.

113

COAL HARBOUR
"A WHALE OF A TOWN"

ORIGINALLY A HARBOUR FOR LOADING COAL, THE COAL OF THE AREA WAS OF SUCH A LOW GRADE IT SOON BECAME UNMARKETABLE WHEN HOLBERG, A MORE NORTHERLY COMMUNITY WAS ESTABLISHED AS A PART OF THE DEW LINE THE AIR FORCE SET UP A BASE AT COAL HARBOUR ERECTING TWO LARGE HANGERS FOR RECONAISSANCE PLANES. THE HARBOUR IS STILL DOTTED WITH EX AIR FORCE BUILDINGS THE OWNER OF THE RED AND WHITE FOOD STORE SHOWED ME THE LINES ON HIS FLOOR REMAINING FROM THE DAYS WHEN IT WAS AN AIR FORCE RECREATION HALL. WHEN THE AIR FORCE LEFT IT BECAME A WHALING STATION. COLORED PHOTOS IN THE RED AND WHITE STORE TELL THE STORY OF A TIME WHEN HUGE WHALES WERE DRAGGED FROM THE OCEAN AND BOTH THE OCEAN AND BEACH WERE RED WITH THEIR BLOOD

JAW BONES OF THE GIANT GREY WHALE.

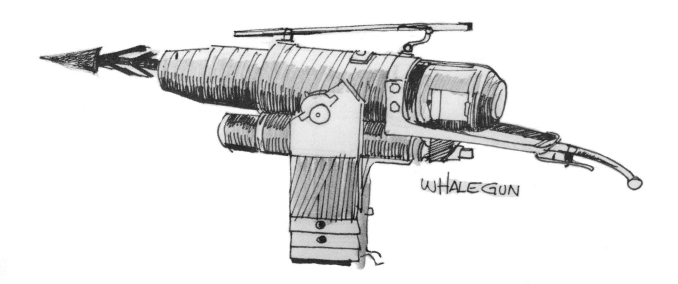

WHALEGUN

COAL HARBOUR

RANGER 81

CAPE SCOTT
HOMESTEAD.

ONE OF THE MANY BUILDINGS
LEFT BEHIND, FIRST BY THE
AIR FORCE AND LATER BY THE
WHALING INDUSTRY.

HOLBERG WAS ORIGINALLY
AN AIR FORCE BASE AND PART
OF THE DEW LINE. A ROAD LEADS
FROM HOLBERG TO THE CAPE
SCOTT PROVINCIAL PARK WHERE
YOU MAY VIEW SEALS, SEA LIONS,
PUFFINS AND MAYBE A POD OF
KILLER WHALES. BE PREPARED
FOR RAIN. THE CAPE RECEIVES
BETWEEN 375 AND 500 CENTI-
METRES ANNUALLY

BE PREPARED
FOR THE
UNEXPECTED

WHEN TRAVELING THE BACKROADS AND INDEED THE MAIN ROADS
OF THE NORTH ISLAND IT IS WELL TO HEED THE SIGNS "REMEMBER
LOGGING TRUCKS HAVE THE RIGHT OF WAY"

LONGHOUSE, ALERT BAY.

LONGHOUSE ALERT BAY.
CORMORANT ISLAND
NEAR PORT McNEILL

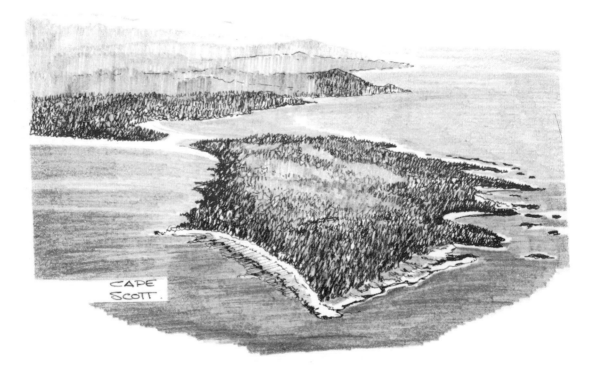

CAPE SCOTT.

CAPE SCOTT
THE NORTH WESTERN
TIP OF CANADAS
"BIG ISLAND"